MW01256799

Dr. Morkos is our most productive faculty member from a clinical standpoint (even while pursuing his master's program!), which I attribute to an incredible reservoir of energy and a complete mastery of the logistics of ambulatory care delivery, documentation, etc. Since joining our faculty, he has suggested multiple ways in which our processes can improve. He has a talent for seeing opportunities for process improvement and a real drive for continuous improvement. We have implemented some of his suggestions for efficiency, and our whole service line has benefitted. Dr. Morkos' clinical productivity is extraordinarily high, outperforming a full-time clinical target by 40%. A master of efficiency, he is always eager to contribute to projects that will improve patient care and/or clinic efficiency. He is highly sought after by his primary care colleagues.

— (MELISSA CAVAGHAN, MD, SERVICE LINE LEADER, DIVISION OF ENDOCRINOLOGY AND METABOLISM, INDIANA UNIVERSITY SCHOOL OF MEDICINE)

I am always very impressed with Dr. Morkos. He faces me when he speaks (even as he enters info into the computer), asks my opinions, encourages me, and asks for questions. I feel that he is thorough and proactive. Thank you, Dr. Morkos!

— *(ANONYMOUS PATIENT REVIEW, INDIANA UNIVERSITY HEALTH)*

Dr. Morkos is extremely efficient in the clinic.

— *(MICHAEL ECONS, MD, CHAIR OF THE DIVISION OF ENDOCRINOLOGY AND METABOLISM, INDIANA UNIVERSITY SCHOOL OF MEDICINE)*

Dr. Morkos is a very organized physician and always has a plan and a backup plan for most situations. He is an actual investigator, always with excellent clinical reasoning and a very reasonable approach for every patient. He is a very good teacher and has excellent skills for teaching. It has been a great pleasure to work with Dr. Morkos, and he has been a really good teacher, senior resident, and friend. He's always wondering how to help the team. He is a very smart and a nice person.

— *(ANONYMOUS RESIDENT FEEDBACK, JOHN H. STROGER JR. HOSPITAL OF COOK COUNTY, CHICAGO, IL)*

NO WORK AFTER HOURS

TOOLS TO MAINTAIN A PLEASANT, EFFICIENT, AND PRODUCTIVE CLINIC WITHOUT WORK BEFORE OF AFTER HOURS

MD EFFICACY
BOOK 1

MICHAEL MORKOS, MD

Dedication

My wife, Sandy, your abundant love and continuous guidance shaped me into a much better version of myself. Thanks for keeping up with me and my endless ambitions.

My sons, Daniel and Anthony, you're the ultimate source of joy in my life. You taught me how to rearrange my priorities and focus on what matters most.

My parents, your continued belief, and your investment in me are why I am who I am today. Words won't suffice for your unlimited love and sacrifices.

CONTENTS

INTRODUCTION

Recognizing a problem doesn't always bring a solution, but until we recognize that problem, there can be no solution.
(James A. Baldwin)

Through the years, I noticed many physicians overwhelmed due to their clinical needs. Many needed to catch up in the clinic, with heavy loads of late documentation and unanswered inbox messages. As I observed my mentors in their clinics, I noticed simple electronic health record (EHR) navigation skills needed to improve. I saw a massive potential for improvement.

There are several critical things we don't get to learn till becoming attending clinicians. Medicine is a diverse and rich field, and our impact on patients can be substantial. We chose to pursue a path to be a part of the healing of sick people. There's a lot to learn in medicine. This is why we have medical schools, residency, and fellowship programs.

By graduation, the medical fund of knowledge is usually outstanding. There's a steep learning curve to be an independent clinician in the first year of an attending's life. Afterward, doctors are generally comfortable in the medical practice.

On the other hand, there may be minimal in-depth understanding of many other practice-related aspects and discomfort with the business practice of medicine. Some business and management topics may include efficiency, productivity, patient satisfaction, managing employees, workflow management, self-consciousness, understanding the best career fit, and respecting family needs. The result may be working before or after hours, lower income, burnout, career shifts later in life, poor patient satisfaction reviews, or frequent empty slots.

In this series of books, MD Efficacy, I'll tackle the above-mentioned issues from a clinician's standpoint, one at a time. Enjoy the read, and more to follow!

1

EFFICACY IS IMPORTANT

Efficiency is doing things right; effectiveness is doing the right things.
(Peter Drucker)

There is a considerable difference between efficiency and effectiveness. We may be running fast, but the running course is a very different consideration. You want to choose the right direction upfront, and then you can run as fast as you want. Efficacy is an excellent word to combine both terms in one.

A Life to Enjoy

Our lives are rich and there are many aspects for us to enjoy. The academic success and career path is one crucial aspect. As physicians, we are high-level achievers. We dedicated many hours to study and training and maintain our work as a high priority. The nature of our work is critical as it directly impacts lives. We must be attentive since a mistake can come with an expensive toll.

The family is a great source of joy and support. Initially, the family origin and, later on, spouse and children constitute our closest and most important social circle. We are social creatures by nature and were designed to live in societies. Like anything else, societal relationships come with obligations that require time and attention. For example, when visiting a sick family member or planning to attend a marriage ceremony, you must think about it, schedule the time and what you need to get, and postpone other things you could have done.

Engagement in the community is another nourishing aspect. This includes religious and social communities. As a

Christian, I'll use the church as an example of a religious institution. Activity in the community builds an altruistic part in our personalities and promotes service. This will mostly be unpaid service based on its voluntary nature. Yet, it can consume a lot of time because you love it and feel the value of your actions. It can also be very influential in your life like it is in mine. I am actively involved in several leadership positions at my church. My service significantly shaped my personality towards a better version of myself, and it continues to do so.

Attending to yourself is another essential aspect, and nourishing your spirit, soul, emotions, and body is crucial. It would be best to dedicate the time for that, plan it, and ensure it will be performed as intended. This means an additional margin to your busy schedule.

As we explore different interests and hobbies, we will likely find great value in these activities. Some may find music, painting, singing, writing, moviemaking, and podcasting, among many others, as a calling to make an impact in others' lives. There is much to enjoy in life for us and others.

Your Presence is Important

You are a critical aspect in many places. Of utmost priority, you are most vital to your family. No one can replace your role there. This is also where your impact is the strongest. We live in an era of career achievement with an unstoppable potential. This is great from one perspective, but it can also mean dismissing the family. Remember that each person's time is limited, so you may overlook others if you dedicate too much time to one area.

I am a big believer that each physician should have a unique niche. The more focused you are on a specific aspect, the more you will know about all the ins and outs, and the more you will provide the best service for your patients. From another perspective, as medicine is institutionalized everywhere with shrinking solo private practices, you want to be unique at your work. We are replaceable at work. Building something you are so good at and well-known for will establish your position in your institution. This takes time, effort, and dedication, but it is worth it.

As you put everything together, imagine your life as a house. You would like your house to be beautiful inside and out. You will never see a beautiful house as a single wall only, right? This doesn't make a lot of sense. The same applies to our lives. If it's work only, the single wall of career is well-done, but nothing else. This house is deficient and imbalanced. If my career wall is for a skyscraper, but the family, community, and personal walls are for a 1-story house, this is very imbalanced. I prefer to build it one story at a time. It will take time, but it is well-balanced. If you want to go fast, you may end up going alone. But if you want to go with your loved ones, you need to slow down and trust me, you will go even further.

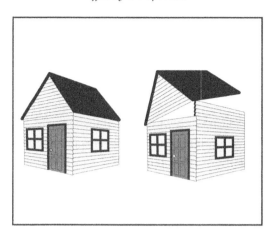

The last thing we want is a broken family or a similar undesirable consequence while having a great career success. Luckily, these things are predictable and preventable if we have the right priorities, awareness, and vigilance.

Why Clinical Efficacy?

There is a lot to enjoy in life, which means having time and dedication. Another area for improvement is having adequate revenue from the clinical work, considering we are in a high-earning field. Our time is valuable and well-paid. You want to work enough hours to earn a good income while maintaining your sanity and having reasonable hours afterward to do your other responsibilities and leisure activities.

I noted unlucky and repetitive trends throughout the years with many of my colleagues. Many would like to have higher incomes and maximize their revenue. They will work longer hours and subsequently have a much higher inbox load. The technical skills in the electronic health record

(EHR) and the ability to set good boundaries are not optimal for many clinicians. The outcome is working for at least a couple of hours, frequently more, before or after the patient-contact hours, to finish the many other tasks. And sometimes worse, working over the weekends when they are not on-call to catch up with the unfinished work. This may significantly interfere with family life and other commitments, and these hazy boundaries can have undesirable consequences.

Another trend for some physicians is to complain about deficiencies but not work on improving their skills or being the change agents in their work environments. There's always a space for self-improvement and helping ourselves and others to improve. As to the EHRs, they have added a lot of value as compared to the old paper-based records. This includes access to various specialty notes, labs, imaging studies with the actual images, order placement, and prescriptions at a glance from anywhere in the world. Despite all these added values, we mostly keep complaining about them, sometimes for good reasons, but don't put in the necessary effort to utilize them to the maximum potential.

Productivity

Your income is important as you most likely have loans that you need to pay. You also worked hard through the years and deserve a good living. Although projected compensation was probably a significant factor in your specialty decision, the charge you're placing with every patient is how you'll achieve this goal.

Medicine is a humane job since we care for sick patients. We're lucky to be physicians. It's a real honor, and we should all take pride in what we're doing on a daily basis. This is also a paid job, and we should understand its business aspects very well. Otherwise, you may be missing out on a lot.

Even though revenue is a significant reason for many physicians to pick their lifetime specialty, many physicians don't understand the fine details of how to obtain this revenue. Many will underbill to avoid audits but overwork to maintain their income. Also, workflow assessment and reengineering can sometimes make a significant impact. These are skills we didn't get to learn at any phase of our medical education.

I could dedicate a whole book to addressing productivity details from a practicing physician's standpoint. There's a lot to share and know so that you can reach your maximum potential during your business hours.

I hope you will have a fruitful life filled with joy and accomplishments in many aspects. I would like you to be very effective at work, utilizing the work hours to their maximum potential. You spend adequate time with your patients, achieve the wanted clinical outcomes, finish your inbox and clinical duties during work hours, and go home with no overdue work. This will allow you all the time you desire for yourself, your family, community service, and anything else you would like to do.

Strategic planning for your life is crucial. What is your calling? What are you here for? How do you want to split your time? These are questions for you, and you only can answer them. I will do my best in the upcoming chapters to help you to be very efficient in your clinic. You may also visit www.MDEfficacy.com and sign up for the newsletter for other tips and tricks. When you combine the right vision, mission, and efficiency, efficacy exists.

MD Efficacy

Efficient at work
Complete your work during the workday

Effective in your personal time
Develop solid relationships and build community

2

INVEST IN LEARNING YOUR EHR

Small changes can lead to remarkable results over time.
(Atomic Habits by James Clear)

Big Systems

I got a call from a friend of mine, an endocrinologist who trusted in my informatics and computer skills. She had her screen zoom at 75% to fully navigate all the EHR capabilities on her laptop screen, which is smaller than the regular monitor. She talked to the Helpdesk, who escalated it to a higher rank, but they were stuck because they didn't have wider laptop screens. As she spoke to me and we had a video call, I showed her a simple trick: instead of using the plus and minus buttons, which go in 25% increments, type the zoom percentage, a simple and basic functionality. She kept escalating the number up to 96%, and the joy filled her heart. It was much better, and her problem was solved. A practicing clinician's skills bring significantly different expertise than the computer experts. Although their input is valuable, it's different.

The EHR systems have grown significantly in the past decade after implementing the HITECH Act with its bonuses and penalties. The complexity of these systems increased as well. They're no longer the basic interfaces with patient information, notes, labs, and medications. They have many tabs and massive databases, capturing patient and user details.

Like everything in life, every option comes with advantages and disadvantages. These large systems have the benefit of having extraordinary capabilities in many tasks. They are impressive since they can take care of the outpatient, inpatient, pharmacy, labs, radiology PACS, cardiology PACS, and pathology. They also provide great potential for analytics, both for research and operational purposes. On the other hand, they can get complicated, and the average user may know a minimal portion of their relevant system's capabilities.

Here is a more specific example of a user working with only a minimal portion of a broadly capable system. Imagine the drive from your new house to work. There's a direct route that only takes 10 minutes. When you initially opened your Maps application, it also showed the other potential paths, including one 25 minutes away. If you didn't check the app beforehand and someone previously showed you the 25-minute way as the sole option, it may be the only one you would ever follow. Fifteen minutes is not a big deal if it's a single instance. But if you drive it twice daily, every business day, that would be a waste of 2.5 hours per week and around 120 hours yearly.

Core Aspects

For any sophisticated computer application, there are core aspects you need to know and shortcuts for the more talented users to quicken the processes. For example, in my current version of Cerner, there's a (Provider View) designed to be the home page, and I can get everything done from there. It was initially intended to be in 3 panes: the left side for the navigation menu, the middle for all the data, and the third for documentation. The middle pane will include the documents, allergies, histories, labs, imaging studies, pathology reports, and charges. The third pane can be created by clicking on the (move) button for the text boxes of the history of the present illness, review of systems, physical exam, ... etc. If you do it that way, you can navigate to where you want by the left and middle panes and write what you need in the right pane, all on a single screen. It's beautiful when you set it right. The problem is that it's not pre-set, and you need to arrange it manually in the correct order that matches your workflow. I had to set it for many of those working close to me, and they enjoyed it when feeling the improvement it made in their daily lives.

You should know how to write notes, place orders, and send scripts. You should also get authorized to prescribe controlled substances, send messages to other providers, communicate electronically with your staff, and place charges. Sometimes, you need a third-party link or app, and the informatics team should set you up. These are core functionalities in the EHR; these aren't tips for a tech-savvy guru. It necessitates focus during the orientation sessions to ensure getting them right.

Programmers and Helpdesk employees could be better, and so could we. The EHR may need to be set up better when you start using it. Those teaching you how to use it may not provide the most efficient ways upfront. Sometimes, the Helpdesk resolution for your concerns may need to be revised. Please don't take their advice for granted and continue to investigate and improve your workflow independently. Continue to voice your concerns, for this is how systems improve.

EHR Workflow

It was interesting to study workflow management during my preparation for the board exam in clinical informatics. Different doctors may have vastly different workflows. Some would like to start with the labs and imaging studies, while others would like to start with the scheduled appointments and documents. The default setting for your EHR may not match what you're doing with every patient. The good thing is that you will set it once, and this will take care of 95% of it. Minor adjustments in the future can happen, but they likely won't be drastic.

It would be best to learn how to change the order and simulate what you'll do from opening the chart until you finish your note and close. Re-order the different workflow components to match them.

For example, here is mine in the order I do it for the left-sided menu and middle (content) panes:

- Chief Complaint
- Care Recommendations (quality metrics)
- Visits List (prior and upcoming clinic visits)
- Problem List
- Documents
- Home Medications
- Opioid Review
- Allergies, Histories (for surgeries, past, family, and social histories)
- Vital Signs
- Labs
- Radiology
- Pathology
- Clinical Media (to insert pictures)
- Order Entry
- Order Profile (previously-ordered studies)
- Outstanding Orders (pending labs)
- Clinical Charge Entry

My order for the third pane (where I document the note):

- History of Present Illness
- Review of Systems
- Physical Exam
- Assessment and Plan

- Diagnostics
- Procedures

This is an example of a logical and reasonable workflow, at least for me. Please think about yours and dedicate the time upfront to get it settled. If you notice after a few days that some things need improvement and reassortment, that's a healthy sign since it indicates that you're more aware of your workflow. It'll take a few minutes at the moment but can save you much more in the future.

Auto-Texts and Smart Phrases

It's nice that we tend to do the same things repeatedly. The more effective your routine is, the more efficient you will be. It is the same as teachers who usually say the same things. One significant difference distinguishing the skilled is how well they prepare their lesson. Similarly, how a clinician establishes their routine determines how efficient and effective they can be.

I frequently save two types of data for future use. The first is the things I often type, like history elements, physical exams, reviews of systems, plans, or patient instructions. The second is the lengthy instructions, even if infrequent, that may consume much time to retype. These are called auto-texts in Cerner and smart phrases in Epic, but I need clarification on other systems. For example, history for thyroid nodules, instructions on how to take levothyroxine, my template for continuous glucose monitor interpretation, and diabetes target instructions for patients are among the commonly used ones. As you'll see later in the patient encounter chapter, I always have written instructions for my patients to decrease miscommunication and reliance on memory. I occasionally order 24-hour urine testing and have saved a paragraph for that. These templates make life a bit easier, and I continue to edit and improve them as needed.

It is not too difficult to insert customizations in your pre-written templates. For example, in Cerner, you can place an underscore "_" where you want to edit the information in your auto-texts and toggle between them by "F3". In Epic, you can put asterisks "***" in your smart phrases and use F2 to toggle between them. This makes life much easier in filling the customizable parts of your templates. If you use the mouse every time you want to modify a part of a template, you'll likely miss some, and it'll take more time. Make sure to mark all the areas that need to be modified, especially those containing modifiable data like gender, pronouns, and the ones you need to update.

Preferred Orders

Following the same train of thought, we tend to order the same things all the time. If you're searching every time for orders, this is a big waste of precious time. Learn how to create your favorite lists and do them well. You do them once, and it will help you tremendously. For example, in my endocrinology world, I have favorite folders for thyroid, diabetes, adrenal, pituitary, and bones, among several others. I go to each folder, and all the lab and special script orders are there.

Order Sets

Several diseases for each specialty have a preset of labs and imaging studies to be done routinely. For example, in MEN 1, I order 15-20 labs and imaging studies annually. It's best for these types of orders to be compiled in an order set and all these orders to be pre-checked. It'll take just a couple of clicks to place the orders rather than the mental and physical burden of sorting them together every time. This can save a significant amount of time. Your clinical informatics specialist or champion can help you build these care sets, which are definitely worth the time and effort.

Tech-Savvy Users

There's a big difference, at least in my mind, between knowing tips and tricks to make your life easier in the clinic versus being innately curious to explore and navigate technology. Through the years, my tech-savvy mentors and friends tended to dig deeper and explore the EHR. They came out with exciting tips and handed them to end-users on a plate of gold. I want to say here that you don't need to be tech-savvy, but you do need to know where to go. Be open to modifying your workflow by including and trying these tips.

We were born with different talents and skill sets. You don't need to be tech-savvy to be efficient, but get to know tech-savvy friends and be keen on learning from them. The IT staff, who provide onboarding to the physicians, can provide some fundamental insights and an introduction to how to use the EHR. But to go into practical workflow tips, it's best to get them from an efficient practicing clinician. If I were in your shoes, I'd identify the most efficient clinician where you are and ask them for a presentation (or a series of them) on improving clinical efficiency and EHR utilization. Another option is to shadow them during a half-day clinical, which will be a practical mentorship. The workflow lessons you learn can be precious in your daily practice.

Status Quo Bias

Humans are not big fans of change, and we tend to develop a routine and love sticking with it. It gives comfort to the brain and limbic system. You know the famous quote: 'Why rock the boat?' That's why many people write about managing change and dealing with resistance, a daily struggle in leadership. Your routine will determine how efficient you are. If I were in your shoes, I'd consciously combat stagnation, inertia, and preference to stay where you are. Going through the pains of change can help you improve your routine. You'll eventually have a steady state that is a more efficient one.

Explore

I encourage you to take the lead and start discovering your EHR system. From a programmer's standpoint, they want to make the system user-friendly, easy to navigate, and comprehensive to cover your needs. As you start checking different menus and buttons, you'll likely be impressed with the new things you discover and how simple things can save you a lot of time. Don't underestimate saving 30 seconds per patient when multiplied by the number of patients you see per week, month, and year.

In Cerner (my current EHR), when I was playing around under the options menu while in the documents, I discovered that you could default the collapsing of certain note types. I specified the outpatient endocrine notes, phone notes, and discharge summaries. This made my life far more manageable when I wanted to see who last saw the patient, when it was, and if the patient got admitted to the hospital.

As part of workflow management, I frequently look at the details of the scheduled visits, who scheduled them, and when they happened. The beauty of the EHR is that everything gets logged. This is under (Action history), but for whatever reason, it's the 15th in the order of the tabs. You need to click 15 clicks on the 'right' button to get there. When I went there, I kept looking for its options and eventually got it to be the first tab. When I shared this with my nurse lead, she was so grateful and regretted her time doing the 15 clicks with every patient in the last seven years. This was a core part of her daily routine with every patient.

When you start exploring various options, you'll begin to have questions and concerns, and this is when you start using the informatics people who are trying to help you in your clinic. Computer systems are always on the move, so try to participate in this movement. Your concerns will be considered if legitimate, and your life may get a bit easier. After the introduction of the ability to upload images to our notes, it was a significant improvement. After a while, the 'Browse' option was not working; I couldn't upload the image files for my ultrasound pictures. I submitted a

Helpdesk ticket, and that plug-in had a code error. They promised to fix it with the following upgrade, and they did. It was great, but I doubt it would be corrected if it wasn't pointed out.

Insulin pumps and continuous glucose monitors (CGMs) are the bread and butter of an endocrinology practice. That's what we do for many patients daily in the clinic. During my training as a fellow, I got exposure to a single type of insulin pump, and the nursing staff were the ones pulling the report. I had no clue how to do it. Everything was coming my way when I started practicing after fellowship, and I had to learn them.

However, many staff members needed to improve with technology, and the clinic workflow was challenging for me and my more experienced peers. You have one of two options: continue the frustrating situation and keep complaining, or work on finding a solution. I asked the clinic manager and got access to all the online accounts for all these devices. I spent significant time understanding how to upload and link the patients' devices. Eventually, I developed a cheat sheet document for all the clinic staff to download all the reports. While several of my colleagues are challenged by new staff members who are still learning, I can directly access and download whatever reports I need in less than a minute. Life can get much more manageable if you know how to do it. I'm not advocating that you don't teach your MA or nurse how to do it. I keep educating them while ensuring that my clinic is flowing well.

Know How for No Lost Time

There are many aspects of the patients' workflow that we don't do. I don't check in the patients, schedule patients, log vital signs, transcribe outside labs, pull the various device reports, check out patients, or do the prior authorizations. I truly appreciate the staff members who work hard on these things so that I can focus on medicine without distractions.

Yet, your life will be significantly affected if you don't know how to do them and the assigned person decides to leave without prompting or on an unexpected time off. I learned how to be curious and learn the details of everyone's work. I'll observe, try it myself, and learn how to do it. I'll remain firm that I won't do others' jobs routinely, as everyone is accountable for their own work. But everyone knows that I'm competent to do it all. For the CGMs and insulin pumps, I know how to upload all the devices myself. Staff members will come to me if they attempt to download them and fail. I'll take care of it only in these instances.

I also believe in continuous education for me and the staff. I'm always learning something new from them and continue to teach and support them to grow in their roles. I won't take the short path of doing it myself instead of taking the time to teach them and correct their mistakes. It's an investment that you'll pay upfront. If you spend the time, they'll make your life much easier.

MD Efficacy

Efficient at work
Lifelong learning of tips and tricks, on your own and from others, to maximize EHR utilization

Effective everyday
Develop skills for self-reliance and to support others

3

TYPING SKILLS

The only way to get better at something is to do it.
(Mark Manson)

Touch typing, typing on the keyboard without looking at the letters, wasn't familiar during my upbringing. None of my teachers, mentors, or colleagues ever mentioned it. While preparing for the clinical skills certification exam, I was concerned about the time limitation for writing the notes in the exam and decided to learn touch typing. As I was studying for the clinical knowledge United States Medical Licensing Examination (USMLE) exam, my time availability was limited. So, I dedicated 20 minutes per day and chose the first website that came up on Google. Despite the frequent frustrations, I was consistent with the daily practice. Over two months, a drastic change happened and I could touch type. At that time, my typing speed was 20-25 words per minute, and now I'm at around 50-60 words per minute. It helped me dramatically in several aspects of my practice.

Clinical Encounter

I'm a big fan of finishing my note during the clinical encounter with the patient. When the patient leaves, I'm done with my note and have signed it. I'll elaborate on the specifics of that in the upcoming chapters. As I got better skilled in touch typing, I could type the note while looking the patient in the eyes, focus on the content, and type while talking and listening. It's comparable to having a scribe; the only difference is that the one typing is the doctor rather than someone who doesn't have the same expertise. This ensures having high-quality, effective communication while continuing to maintain clinical efficiency.

Scribing

The thought of having a scribe was raised several times in our departmental meetings. Besides their cost, the main concern was the quality of the notes. My wife, a primary care doctor, was skeptical until she got the scribe. After initial resistance, the scribe idea was implemented, making her life much better and less stressful. The quality of the notes is not the same anymore, but she is okay with that compromise and glad to improve her clinic workflow. It just depends on your priorities and how careful you are about what's written in the notes. It may not be worth it if editing every note takes an additional 5-10 minutes. If you're efficient in writing your notes, it may not add that much saved time. Maybe it won't be worth the expense, technical hassles, and lower documentation quality.

Dictation

Dictation is another approach for composing the note. It's faster to speak than to type on a keyboard. I think that it can be useful in some instances. I will consider it while doing the inbox and writing a relatively long message. It'll save time in this uncommon circumstance. For the day-to-day use, I have several arguments against its routine use. Dictating the note means waiting until the visit is over and re-stating all the findings, including the history, review of systems, physical exam, and assessment and plan. This is a lot to recall and can consume 5-10 minutes after every visit. If I am behind in the clinic, and the notes of several visits get postponed, whatever I retain is far less, and leaving the clinic will be delayed due to this unfinished work. This is not good for documentation quality or a healthy work-life balance. Dictation can have spelling mistakes, and you may need to re-read what was written by the natural language processing (NLP) algorithm that analyzed what you dictated. Like other artificial intelligence programs, NLP algorithms can have issues understanding some accents. They improve with time but are not perfect (neither are we). When I'm dictating, I prefer a headset or a mic so that my hands are free to type when I need to correct the misspelled words. Dictating via a handheld piece or phone will prevent the ability to type these corrections and add more wasted time going back and forth with the dictation device.

Admin

Many physicians evolve within administrative roles, and I'm blessed to have several at my church. As the secretary of my church's board of trustees and the previous secretary (coordinator) of the high school service, I keep all the notes of these meetings, which sometimes can be extensive. Touch typing allowed me to guide the conversations and actively discuss my points while typing the essential aspects. Usually, by the time I finish these meetings, I'm done with the meeting minutes. I'll proofread them quickly and send them right afterward; it's incredible how fast you can get things done. The other beautiful thing is that there's no delay in sending the documents (especially if you tend to forget) and that you didn't take time away from your family or other important things you were planning to do.

Keyboard Shortcuts

The EHR is the standard tool to document nowadays, meaning you're dealing with computers all day in the clinic. I'll assume you're unfamiliar with the keyboard shortcuts, so I can share much of what I know. From a young age, I got intrigued by the keyboard shortcuts written beside the corresponding functionality in various menus. Trying 'Ctrl + o' and a new window or document pop-up was fun. A law in informatics called Fitt's law mentions that the amount of time needed for the user to move the cursor from its current position to the target is defined by the distance to the target divided by the target's size. Moving the mouse from where it is to the desired target will take some time. That time will multiply by how often you use it for that specific goal. When you use a keyboard shortcut, you don't need to consider that time as the action happens immediately. It sounds very appealing, but it can get overwhelming when you know how many shortcuts exist. I recommend focusing on learning the most used shortcuts to bring you the highest impact, and you can add others slowly. The following keyboard short-cuts will apply to Windows computers, as Mac computers are slightly different. Since most computers in various insti-tutions are Windows, I'll cover those to decrease confusion. I'll underline the key letters, whenever available, to remind you of the shortcuts. For example, (Ctrl + o: open), the (o) is present in the word (open), so I'll underline it this way: open, note the underlined o.

Keyboard shortcuts

- *Ctrl + c: Copy*
- *Ctrl + v: Paste*

- *Ctrl + x: Cut (Note that x, c, and v are beside each other)*
- *Ctrl + a̱: Select a̱ll*
- *Ctrl + z: Undo*
- *Ctrl + y: Redo (Note that y and z are subsequent letters)*
- *Ctrl + ḇ: Ḇold*
- *Ctrl + u̱: U̱nderline*
- *Ctrl + i̱: I̱talics*
- *Shift + arrow: Highlight in that direction*
- *End: Move the cursor to the end of the line*
- *Shift + end: Highlight till the end of the line*
- *Ctrl + end: Move the cursor to the end of the document*
- *Ctrl + shift + end: Highlight till the end of the document*
- *Windows + Shift + s̱: S̱nippet tool for an on-screen picture capture*
- *Ctrl + zero: Fit screen in Acrobat PDF*
- *F2: Rename*
- *Alt + Space + x̱: Max̱imize the window*
- *Alt + F4: Close the window*
- *Ctrl + F4: Close the tab*
- *Alt + ḏ: Select the aḏdress bar*
- *Alt + tab: Select a different application*
- *Tab: Toggle between different text boxes, icons, or spaces*

While navigating the EHR, you may have noticed an underlined letter in the available buttons or menu options. You can usually get there by clicking (Alt + the underlined letter). For example, you may find (Accept) and (Decline) when signing the prescription orders. This means (Alt + a:

Accept) and (Alt + d: Decline). Take your time and focus on the important ones you're using frequently.

If you sign up for the newsletter email list at www.MDEf ficacy.com, you will get a printable single sheet for the commonly used shortcuts for Windows and Mac users. This can be a good reminder for you to practice them. If you are consistent in trying them, they will eventually be second nature.

MD Efficacy

Efficient at work
Touch typing and command keys allow for quick navigation

Effective everyday
Initial time investment to learn pays off daily

4

YOUR NOTE

Good notes are like good maps. They help you navigate
the terrain and find your way to your destination.
(Angela Duckworth)

Physician notes have three main uses: clinical,
billing, and liability.

Clinically, the note is a great source to understand a patient's history, physical exam findings, diagnostics, assessment, and plan. Clinicians communicate with each other via these notes. Having seen hand-written notes previously, I'm so grateful for the current computerized notes because they're easily readable. Also, in the current EHR era, you can quickly go to any specialist's notes and understand their plan, assuming it's a single EHR system for your institution.

From a billing perspective, the insurance companies will pay you based on the CPT charge level codes you submitted. Your documentation determines this. Auditors get paid to find charge errors, and the mistakes can lead to grave outcomes and significant financial penalties. I'm not aiming to scare or encourage you to under-code. It's just a kind reminder to understand the ins and outs of your specialty-specific charges and document what the auditors want to see, word for word, seriously.

Finally, your notes will be crucial in any liability situation. Although unlucky, we may need to defend ourselves in court. An important thing that you would heavily rely on at that time would be your documentation. An analogy would be like talking to an officer if you were ever pulled over in your car. You don't want to speak so much as you might make mistakes. Also, you don't want to talk so little that you don't answer the question you are asked. You need to find that sweet spot.

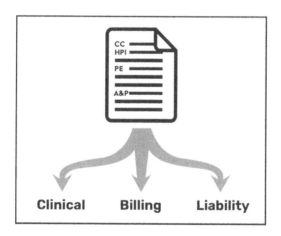

Clinical

The most prolonged notes I ever read are those of medical students. They write many details, including the fine details in stories, even if they're irrelevant to the presentation. Just because the patient said so, they feel the need to document it. As the training years go by, experience increases, and the notes get shorter. Perfection-seeking personalities tend to have lengthy, detailed notes as well.

On the other hand, some physicians have low-quality notes with less beneficial information. You'll be unlucky if you inherit their panel as you try to discern what they thought about or have done for their patients. They may be brilliant, but their notes don't communicate this brightness.

I recommend you develop an effective way of writing the notes that work for you, tackle the three aspects mentioned earlier, and stick with it. I'll share mine here for your reference and feel free to copy whatever benefits you.

- **Chief Complaint**

I always start with the chief complaint, a billing mandate in any note. It answers the essential question: Why are you seeing this patient today? Example: "Follow up for type 2 diabetes".

- **History of Present Illness**

Afterward is the history of the present illness (HPI). I always start with a one-liner. A made-up example: Mr. Smith is a 65-year-old man with a history of type 2 diabetes, hypertension, dyslipidemia, and multinodular goiter presenting for managing type 2 diabetes and multinodular goiter. It usually reminds me of the bigger picture, and I continue to expand it as newer issues arise.

During the initial visit, I will gather the relevant data about the patient's history. Some diseases have clear, specific checklists that will include most of the relevant information. In the endocrinology world, these include diabetes, hyperthyroidism, thyroid cancer, primary hyperparathyroidism, osteoporosis, and obesity. As you can imagine, I have auto-texts for them. So, from the 2nd visit and afterward, the history obtained in the initial encounter will be labeled (Initial history + date of the initial visit mm/yyyy), for example, (Initial history 7/2022). The history for subsequent visits will be under (Interval History). If important information were mentioned previously, I'd put it in a date parenthesis after the (Initial History). For example, (3/2023) The patient sustained a fragility hip fracture after tripping over the sidewalk. My general rule is that I'll only look at my last note, and it'll keep all the relevant data about the patient.

- **History and Physical Exam**

There are two ways to log the remaining history elements: past medical history, allergies, family history, social history, and procedures. You can log them in the EHR, each in its corresponding tab, or free text them in your note. When you log them in the EHR once, they will auto-populate with every future note. I maintained the routine of updating them in the EHR. I'm helping my colleagues with their future notes. The note is cleaner as the information will be in the relevant tabs, and you'll be happy when others do it for you. It creates a supportive culture. Keep the review of systems and physical exam findings focused on what's relevant to the patient's presentation. Since the 2021 billing regulation by the Centers for Medicare and Medicaid Services (CMS), there's no longer a billing mandate on the number of elements in either.

- **Investigational studies**

For the patient workup, including labs, imaging studies,

and pathology, it's critical to include the relevant information and what you reviewed. Signing your note, including the pre-populated studies, implies that you reviewed and acted on them. For example, as an endocrinologist, I won't include a platelet count of 20k in a patient with severe thrombocytopenia since I won't act on it, and hematology will follow it. I'm not ignoring the patient's wholeness, but I also know my limitations and defer to the other experts when it's not my field.

I believe in including images; they speak more than 1,000 words. I review the photos of all my related radiology studies and the trends of various labs or findings, take snippets, and insert them in the notes. I don't include the whole reports for imaging studies or pathology reports, but rather the relevant summarizing sentences only. So, the note will be comprehensive yet concise and readable. The clinicians are busy and want to grasp the critical information and continue their busy schedules.

On the other hand, I will discuss the incidental imaging and lab findings with the patients and clearly document them along with the responsible provider to address them. Unaddressed incidental findings can lead to grave problems, patient dissatisfaction, and potential lawsuits.

- **Assessment and Plan (A&P)**

The medical decision-making section is the most important in the note. Some physicians prefer to keep it at the top as this is where the money is. By that, I mean that the most precious information is there and that it's the core of billing and coding. Thinking about the decision-making ladder, you must start from the first step to reach the top. Using the same analogy, I prefer to start with the HPI and end with the assessment and plan, so I also keep it that way in my notes.

My first line would match the billing requirement (CMS 2021 guidelines): Is the problem acute or chronic? Is it well controlled, uncontrolled, not at goal, or is there a severe exacerbation? It's beneficial clinically and for the coding requirement.

Afterward, I think about it as if I'm building a case for the diagnosis. I start with the objective findings in the history sequence, physical exam findings, lab results, imaging studies, and pathology. Then, I move to my analysis to assess the differential diagnosis and what I made from it. Afterward, I'll plan for additional labs, imaging studies, and treatment. I typically don't write with paragraphs as they're not easily readable. I use short bullet points, brief and direct. I keep a white space between the separate sections to make it easier for the reader and myself to grasp the different sections at a glance.

We frequently have plans to repeat certain labs or imaging studies in a specific time interval. I suggest using specific date intervals (like month/year) in your note rather than durations. Writing every note from scratch is impractical, and you don't want to lose track of the dates and your plan due to a lack of specificity. If it's August 2023 and you plan to repeat labs in 6 months, don't write (Repeat labs in 6 months), but rather (Repeat labs in 2/2024). When you copy your note, the date you type will remind you of your initial plan.

- **Example A&P – New Patient**

Here's an example of a note for a patient who is presenting for an initial assessment of thyrotoxicosis (new patient)

- *Newly diagnosed, uncontrolled.*
- *Symptoms started 5/2023, including heat intolerance, sweating, palpitations, tremors, and unintentional weight loss of 20 Ibs.*
- *Initial physical exam showed tachycardia, tremors, and no evidence of exophthalmos.*
- *Initial labs 7/2023: TSH <0.01, free T4 4.5, total T3 450, performed by the primary care physician.*
- *I personally did a spectral Doppler ultrasound in 8/2023, with a peak systolic velocity of 80 cm/sec in the right inferior thyroid artery, consistent with the diagnosis of Graves' disease. There were no notable nodules.*

- *Check thyroid stimulating immunoglobulin today to establish a baseline.*

- *Start methimazole 40 mg daily.*
- *I discussed the risks of allergy, joint pains, hepatotoxicity, and agranulocytosis.*
- *Let me know immediately if you are pregnant.*
- *Follow up in 9/2023 (4-week interval) with labs a few days before the visit.*

The bullet points and logical sequence of reasoning will help the reader to scan through fast and get to what they want efficiently. It will also show them how you reached your conclusion. If you're in a teaching institution, it's a great way of teaching your trainees how to think and come to a reasonable differential and conclusion. I wrote these critical parts of the assessment and plan during the initial encounter, which will continue in future notes. I'll modify it as needed, but the foundation is the same; it saves a lot of time and effort with the follow-ups. Also note the white space between the initial part of the assessment, the plan, and the discussion about therapy's risks and side effects. It helps the reader's brain understand, at a glance, that there are three sections so they can quickly glance through whatever is less relevant and focus on the more important part.

- **Example A&P – Established Patient**

Here's an example of the assessment and plan for a patient presenting to follow up for Graves' disease

- *Chronic, well controlled.*
- *Symptoms started 10/2022, including retrobulbar eye pain, palpitations, and heat intolerance.*
- *Initial labs 12/2022: TSH <0.01, free T4 2.3, total T3 290, thyroid stimulating immunoglobulin (TSI) 5.0*

- *Spectral Doppler US 12/2022 consistent with Graves' disease. There were no notable nodules.*

- *Methimazole dosing:*

12/2022 20 mg daily (-> TSH <0.01, free T4 1.1, total T3 120)
1/2023 10 mg daily (-> TSH 0.4, free T4 0.4, total T3 80)
3/2023 5 mg daily (-> TSH 1.4, free T4 1.0, total T3 120, TSI 3.0)

- *I discussed the risks of allergy, joint pains, hepatotoxicity, and agranulocytosis.*
- *Let me know immediately if you are pregnant.*
- *Repeat TSI in 12/2023 (6-month interval)*
- *Follow up in 9/2023 (3-month interval) with labs a few days before the visit.*

Notice the way the medication dosing and the lab findings are written. It took me some time to get organized from that standpoint. The field of endocrinology is heavily focused on lab findings, and the dose adjustments are based on these labs. This applies to hyperthyroidism, hypothyroidism (levothyroxine dose adjustments), and cabergoline for prolactinoma, among others. I first write the date of the dose adjustment, the dose, and then the labs it led to during the subsequent lab check. The labs will be in brackets with a preceding arrow to show that these labs resulted from that medication adjustment. It helps keep all the dose adjustments in one place and affirms the intention of checking only the last note during patient visits. No previous notes will be checked routinely.

- **Clinical Situations**

For patients who have several uncontrolled problems, it may be overwhelming for the patient and the physician to address all the issues during a single visit. I learned that everyone could get overwhelmed if we cram things up. Focus on the essential items for the patient and discuss your thoughts if an urgent issue needs immediate attention. Then, you can discuss the rest of the problems during a closer visit. I'll still write all the diagnoses and previous assessments to stick with the last note, but I'll write the first line as (Discuss during the next visit, previous plan:).

Some patients tend to have events between the visits, and few may have many of them. Portal messages and, occasionally, phone calls facilitate communication between patients and their physicians. Memory can help you keep track of such events, but it could be unreliable. Documentation is the best objective way of doing so. Going back to my rule, as mentioned earlier, to have the last note as the primary reference, I addend the most recent note with the updates worth keeping. The less important things that won't impact patient care can be dismissed. They will remain in phone notes, but I won't likely review them during patient visits.

- **Summary**

Chief Complaint
Question: Why are you seeing this patient today?
Strategy: Short and focused, it is a billing requirement.
Example: "Follow up for type 2 diabetes"

History Intro
Question: How to remember most of your patient's history upfront?

Strategy: Start with a one-liner. For example: "Mr. Smith is a 65-year-old man with a history of type 2 diabetes, hypertension, dyslipidemia, and multinodular goiter presenting for managing type 2 diabetes and multinodular goiter."

History and Physical Exam
Question: How to keep it concise and comprehensive?
Strategy:
- Label the initial history and keep it in future notes
- Add dates to the important history elements from subsequent visits
- Keep a dedicated area for the interval history. Otherwise, the older history is copied every time
- Write only what is relevant and important

Investigational Studies
Question: What to include?
Strategy: Don't paste the whole reports, but only the relevant and important components

Assessment and Plan
Question: Will your colleagues understand your thought process? Will it stand an audit?
Strategy:
- Start by the facts from the history, physical exam, and investigational studies
- Be explicit in your differential diagnosis and why you considered each
- Be clear in your plan
- Bullet points are much easier to follow as compared to paragraphs
- Use dates rather than time intervals

- Your goal should be to include all the important aspects in your last note, no need to go to the older ones
- Be well-aware of the billing requirements

• **Wrap up**

To summarize the clinical section, the note should be comprehensive to include the relevant data and explicit thought process for the management. The reading clinician should understand the logic of why you came up with the diagnosis and treatment plan. It should also be brief and well-organized so that you sign it by the time you're done with the patient visit; they can navigate it fast and grasp the important aspects at a glance. I'll elaborate on that during the upcoming Patient Encounter chapter.

Billing

Reimbursement in healthcare is getting progressively complicated. The initial simple model was fee-for-service; you pay for what you get. This is shifting to quality-based payments and pre-agreed-upon lump sums for diagnoses and hospital admissions. I'll focus here on the physician-level point of view, as we're the ones who write notes and place charges based on the levels of complexity.

• **Billing Education**

During my fellowship, AACE (American Association of Clinical Endocrinologists, back then) used to hold 2-day intense training courses for billing and coding focused on endocrinologists. I tried to convince my co-fellows and junior attendings to join me in such a course, but I was still waiting for someone to be interested. I don't know if there was an element of shame related to the business aspect of medicine that contradicted its humane mission. The teaching coder for that course considered me a successful student and a promising future coder/auditor. It was fun and I learned a lot.

You need to understand that auditors don't have a medical background. It may be a brief certification after high school or a bachelor's degree. They go with the pre-written rules and may not think twice about them. The rule of thumb is: If it was not documented, it didn't happen. That's why I strongly encourage you to read the specifics to charge for whatever codes you frequently use. Centers for Medicare and Medicaid Services (CMS) publishes them, and I suggest you use the exact phrasing as is. For example, to charge for a continuous glucose monitor interpretation, CMS asks for this phrase: Ambulatory CGM of interstitial tissue fluid via a subcutaneous sensor for a minimum of 72 hours. I have this exact phrase in my template. The data analysis section doesn't have prerequisites, but I have a template for various metrics. Although these are not a requirement, they're important and relevant clinically. It would be best if you met both.

The general idea of coding is similar for outpatient and inpatient services, whether new or established patients. Are they at a low, medium, or high complexity? Based on that, the reimbursement will be determined. These generally follow the normal distribution curve, with most patients in the moderate complexity category and a few in the low and high complexity. Although the rules are pre-defined, most physicians need more under-standing of their ins and outs, and they're frequently under-billing. Few are courageous and over-bill, but the price can be high if they can't defend their charging level in an audit.

- **Billing Examples**

For a patient with type 2 diabetes on insulin who has frequent severe hypoglycemia episodes down to the 40s mg/dL, this is considered a severe exacerbation due to a severe side effect of therapy. We need an objective definition; the American Diabetes Association defines severe hypoglycemia as a serum glucose level <54 mg/dL in its 2023 guidelines. In this specific circumstance, insulin will be regarded as a high-risk medication requiring intense monitoring by frequent glucose checks and a close outpatient follow-up. A close follow-up is defined as within three months by CMS guidelines at the time of writing this book. Therefore, with this single problem, this is considered a high-complexity charge, whether new or established.

Another example is an established patient presenting for the follow-up of Graves' disease. They're well-controlled on methimazole, and I ordered TSH, free T4, and total T3 to be done before the next visit. It's a pleasant short visit and meets the criteria for a medium complexity charge. It can be as short as 5-10 minutes but meets the billing requirement by the medical decision-making.

On the other hand, you may be taking care of ten chronic problems and addressing them. Unless you have criteria meeting the severe exacerbation or high-risk management, this will also be considered a medium complexity problem.

I'm not asking you to compromise the medical care or objectify the patients. But try to reach a middle ground between excellent patient care, reasonable compensation, and avoiding over-working yourself. For example, I'm seeing a patient with diabetes who also wants to discuss her osteoporosis management. She recently got the diagnosis from her primary care physician. It's a reasonable request, but it's a separate visit to allow her the time to understand the pathogenesis and management options of the disease. I'll typically ask her the history details pertinent to osteoporosis, a 5-minute checklist. This will be followed by ordering the labs and x-rays needed to assess it comprehensively, a pre-made order set. Then, I'll ask the patient to arrange a visit in 2-3 weeks after getting them done to discuss the results along with the management options. This allows me to fulfill the patient's need to discuss her diseases in-depth while not overwhelming myself by cramming a 40-minute discussion into a 20-minute slot.

Legal Aspects

Getting notified of a lawsuit can be nerve-wracking and significantly traumatizing. It may be the norm in some states, while it can be rare in others. You must understand the legal climate where you are (or will be) practicing. Also, you should understand your malpractice insurance. What's the cap? And is it covering the usual asks in lawsuits? Or will you have to pay from your earnings on top of their cap and threaten your belongings? Is it per occurrence or claims-based that you'll need tail coverage? And how much will you pay for tail coverage if you leave the current workplace?

Per-occurrence coverage will cover you at any point, even if you moved to a different workplace and state, as long as the incident happened while you were covered. On the other hand, a claims-based policy will cover you as long as you maintain the same coverage and workplace. You're not covered if you move and then get notified about a lawsuit that happened a few days before leaving. It's an exaggeration to give you the idea behind it. After leaving the claims-based policy, you should buy tail coverage to protect yourself. People choose it because it's cheaper, but tail coverage can get expensive. You need to understand the details before signing the contract.

I'll encourage you to read the contract in-depth, one sentence at a time, and with the mindset of finding ways of leaving the place before joining them. I remember doing a better job analyzing my contract than the lawyer I paid to review it. They can be helpful, but you need to do your homework and ask the right questions to get the most out of them. Don't underestimate the red flags. If workplace promises weren't written in the contract, they might never happen.

Documentation is essential since it will be reviewed thoroughly. We need reasonable confidence based on our knowledge and expertise. I also prefer to be explicit about discussing the different options with the patients. Don't write a lot, just brief sentences describing the main ideas. We need a middle ground, neither ignoring the legality of our documentation nor ordering every test under the sky to protect ourselves.

Since the Cures Act, patients have access to most of their healthcare records, including most of their physician notes. Be careful to ensure your writing is accurate and not written in offensive language. I trust you always do that, but it's worth mentioning. Human nature is complicated, and many decisions are emotion-based rather than higher-level reasoning. That's why a pleasant physician-patient relationship is essential.

Problems happen, and life is not easy. We should continue doing our best daily despite the challenges. This will help us better deal with stress, and eventually, we will triumph in our paths and help others through difficult times with the power we get firsthand.

MD EFFICACY

EFFICIENT AT WORK
EXCELLENT DOCUMENTATION ALLOWS YOU AND OTHERS TO
EASILY NAVIGATE THE PATIENT INFORMATION

EFFECTIVE EVERYDAY
THOROUGH NOTES EASE CLINICAL, BILLING, AND POTENTIAL
LEGAL CONCERNS

5

PATIENT ENCOUNTER

Excellence is doing ordinary things extraordinarily well
(John W. Gardner)

The patient encounter is the core of clinical physician practices. It's the reason we went to medical school from the very beginning. The excitement and passion for seeing sick patients and helping them on the path of healing was an ambition. As a previous student and a current academic physician (who's learning continuously), I can see the significant improvement in selecting the right questions as the level of expertise improves, starting from a rotating 3rd-year medical student and going through residency, fellowship, junior faculty, and senior faculty. The more expertise you obtain, the fewer questions you ask, and the more focused you are on the relevant data to help make accurate decisions.

Learning Curve

The clinical encounters as a trainee are different from being an attending physician. Initially, a trainee needs to staff every patient with their attending, present the case, discuss the details, and devise a plan. This slows the workflow, but it's a requirement for training good physicians. As the attending, you're the decision-maker, collecting the information, processing it, and making the workup and treatment decisions on the spot.

As a trainee, I pre-charted before the clinic and spent time afterward studying and understanding the various diseases. There were many details I didn't know, and the ambition to learn was on fire. When I finished the fellowship, I thought I was well-trained, and I was partially correct. I was good at what I knew, but several things were new. I didn't realize how little I learned in thyroid ultrasound. Also, initially, I requested three-month follow-ups for patients with Graves' disease, which was incorrect since they needed follow-ups much sooner, or what I like to call a "sooner visit.". I also checked labs between visits and managed medications accordingly, an inefficient habit that I stopped altogether later.

As you can tell, the first year as an attending had a steep and crucial learning curve. Being independent and autonomous is priceless. The basic foundation for all this is that you need to master your business. You should be comfortable in your medical, surgical, procedural, or hybrid specialty. This is a core necessity to be efficient and productive.

Pre-Charting

As a new attending, I pre-charted for the first week before the clinic visits, and that was it. Reviewing the history, labs, imaging studies, and recent provider notes per patient takes a few minutes. Afterward, I draft what I need to keep in my preliminary note. After that initial week of practicing independently, it became a done deal, no more pre-charting. Once a scheduled patient shows up, I'll do the pre-charting. Some patients won't show up, and there'll be no wasted effort.

Events Between Visits

As mentioned, I keep all the details in the established patients' last progress note. If I get notified of events or patient care discussions, I addend the most recent note in real-time with the important updates, so it'll be the sole reference. I copy the last old note into the new note, and whatever new history I get, it'll go under (interval history) including the updates since the previous visit. I don't modify the older history, but it's there for my reference. I briefly review the notes, labs, and imaging studies done since the last visit. Some data will be relevant and valuable. I will also review the diabetic patients' glucose logs or attached PDFs of the CGMs and insulin pumps before going in. I aim to have an excellent idea of their current situation and a suggested plan before entering the room. This whole process usually takes one to five minutes. The more you practice, the faster you get.

Some patients in my practice are relatively complex and have severe events between visits. I have several options for such patients. The first is to have extended visits for them, so I'll still pre-chart right before the visit. Another option is to flag them in the health record, if possible, and pre-chart them specifically before that clinic day. A third option I choose is to swallow the time delay when seeing these patients, as I'll pre-chart right before their visits. Your work-flow will depend on your clinic's setting and the types of patients you see. One of my colleagues is a pituitary diseases expert, and these patients are the core of her practice. She expects to manage several hormonal disorders with each patient, and many will have a constellation of thyroid, adrenal, gonadal, growth hormone, prolactin, and sodium disorders. The regular 40-minute slots for new patients and 20-minute slots for established patients won't fit these needs. So, she wisely chose 60 minutes for new patients and 30 minutes for established patients. This translated to better patient care with the understanding of decreased revenue.

Who's Leading the Visit?

When you enter the exam room, and after the pleasant greeting, an important question arises: Who's leading the flow of the visit? There are three different approaches here; at one end of the spectrum, you can lay back and give the steering wheel to your patient. They'll ask you the impor-tant questions they have on their mind, and hopefully, they'll be happier when you adequately address all of their concerns at the end of the visit. At its other end, you're fully in charge. You have an agenda of all the items you want to discuss to address their health concerns comprehensively. This agenda will keep expanding as much as the quality metrics keep increasing. And a third middle-ground option is to understand their concerns or questions while tackling your agenda.

I think it's obvious what I'd suggest you choose, but let me share my journey as it may be helpful to understand this choice. As a perfectionist, I tend to have a plan for every patient on what they need to get done. For example, in an uncontrolled patient with type 2 diabetes at the beginning of the year, I may consider adjusting the long-acting and short-acting insulin, checking a lab panel, examining their feet, and ensuring they'll get an eye exam soon. Also, I will try to manage their other health issues that I could help with, like uncontrolled hypertension, dyslipidemia, microalbuminuria, and hypothyroidism. I often saw significant challenges like time constraints and the patients' points of view, which frequently didn't align with mine. A nice metaphor that further elaborates on this issue is to imagine four blindfolded people standing by an elephant. The first felt a thin rope that kept moving (the tail). The second felt a vast, smooth surface like a bag with some movement inside (the stomach). The third noticed a wood-like curved piece (a tusk), while the last noted a tree-like trunk (a foot). They all tried to describe the same animal, but each had a very different description. This is what it means to have diverse points of view on the same issue. The beauty of having these various views is that they complete the picture and decrease bias. If a patient disagrees with my opinion, I patiently ask for clarification on their side of the story and try to understand it. We may disagree, but I'll explain my point of view, knowing that it's their health and decision at the end of the day. I let go as long it's not posing a significant risk that I find unacceptable.

I usually start the visit with a smile and ask how they're doing. After the pleasant brief greeting, I'll navigate what they want me to focus on besides discussing their presenting disease. At the end of the discussed plan, I'll ask if there is anything else they want to talk about. This way, I ensure that I fully address the patient's concerns and allow them to have all their questions answered.

Our behaviors have the upper hand in determining our health status. This may be another book discussing the limbic system and how it drives our decision-making. If a patient is not buying into the plan or is not motivated enough, it will likely fail, and the desired outcome won't happen. Therefore, it's critical to actively involve the patients in the plan.

On the other hand, if the patient allowed me to drive the decision, I should have the comprehensive plan and decisions ready as the treating physician. Several patients would ask what I would do if I were in their shoes. In critical scenarios, I have seen some physicians leave the decision entirely to the patient and remain indecisive. This needs to be corrected since we're the ones who have the medical knowledge and reviewed the history, physical exam, and workup. Therefore, based on that understanding, we can best make evidence-based, reasonable decisions. We should make a good decision or study more to clarify the differences between options. It's like a multiple-choice question in the exam where all the answers are close by, but the correct answer is far away from the others. You'll see that when you know the details very well.

Documentation

Different physicians can have many different approaches to documentation. Here are some of the many I saw:

- Sit in front of the computer in the patient's room and look at the screen while talking to the patient. This type of physician is efficient, but many patients won't be pleased. The satisfaction scores may ultimately need improvement, too. Continuous eye contact is critical.
- Talk to the patient throughout the visit and document afterward via typing or dictation. The patients here are frequently happier, but the physicians are usually behind with their documentation and sometimes postpone the notes till the end of the day on busy days when they're already behind. They will reason that patient care is more important than documentation.
- I once saw a physician dictating in front of their patients in the room. Although efficient, I see it as needing to be more professional and interfering with the basics of good communication.

If I don't have all the details written right away, I'll forget them, which can be a big problem. I also like to have good communication with patients. That's why I love touch typing. I'll talk to the patients and maintain eye contact while my hands are typing the notes. Sometimes, I need to look at my screen for a few seconds, like when placing orders or renewing medications. I'll mention it, and I won't be conversing then. I make my best effort to maintain continuous eye contact during active discussions.

To achieve that, I requested an adjustable cart and a laptop in each clinic. My first exposure to these carts was after a spine injury, but it significantly improved my workflow. Sitting comfortably or standing in the exam rooms and facing the patient during clinical encounters would be best. Many room designs need to have the computer set up that way. Commonly, you'll have to rotate your neck 45 to 180 degrees to face the patient while typing on the pre-installed desktop, which is unhealthy for your spine.

Orders

Endocrinology is a lab-heavy specialty, and I can only adjust the many medication doses I manage through the lab results. And frequently, they sway my questions during the clinical encounter. For example, Thyroid Stimulating hormone (TSH) is the most important in hypothyroidism management, and per my institution's lab assay, the reference range is 0.4 – 4.2 mcU/mL. If a patient had a recent TSH of 1.5, the visit would likely be straightforward, and I'd continue the present management. On the other hand, a previously controlled hypothyroid patient presenting with a TSH of 30 mcU/mL may drive me to ask many questions about supplements, compliance, tablet colors, way of taking it, weight changes, and last refill, among several others. That's why I order all the needed future labs during the patient's visit, set their time frame for the next planned visit, and clearly ask the patient to complete the labs before the visit. I provide specific instructions on fasting status, time of the day, and how many days before the visit to get them done based on what labs I'm requesting. Collagen Type I C-Telopeptide and Procollagen 1 Intact N-Terminal Propeptide, bone turnover markers, can take up to 2 weeks to get results at my institution, while TSH and free T4 will take less than 24 hours to be back. Most patients at my practice follow the instructions, and life is far easier for all parties.

I'm happy to have all the needed data during the visit, ask all the relevant questions, and have a clear and detailed plan for the patient. The patient will also be happy to have a clear plan when they leave the office.

Patient Instructions

During my fellowship, I had two mentors who used to write detailed patient instructions. Since I started practicing independently, I have adopted the same pattern and believe it tremendously helps many patients. Patients may need to remember the details I provide during the visit or refresh their memory about the specifics. Going to the print after-visit summary or through the electronic portal, they will find what I wrote for them.

Here's a practical example I wrote to one of my patients, just modified the name

- *Dear Jenny, it was nice to see you again today*
- *Best of luck with the pregnancy plan*

- *Target fasting glucose and before meals: 60-95 mg/dL*
- *Target 1 hour after eating is <140 mg/dL*
- *Target 2 hours after eating is <120 mg/dL*
- *Target A1c <6.5%*
- *A low glucose level is <60*

- *Start Lantus 10 units at bedtime and Humalog 5 units 5-10 minutes before meals*
- *The sliding scale of Humalog based on your glucose level before the main meals:*

<70: Decrease 4 units after treating the low blood sugar
71-100: Decrease 2 units
100-130: Inject the recommended dose
131-180: Add 1 unit
181-230: Add 2 units
231-280: Add 3 units
281-330: Add 4 units
331-380: Add 5 units
>381: Add 6 units

- *Every Sunday and Thursday, if you notice consistent highs after eating (>140 mg/dL), increase the Humalog dose by 2 units. For example, 5 -> 7 units before meals and so on.*
- *Follow up in 5 weeks with consistent Libre use, to be scanned at mealtimes and bedtime*
- *Please get me your eye exam record; you may call the office and ask them to fax it to me, fax #: ****

You can imagine why patients may not remember all these details. Some patients will keep a screenshot of the sliding scale on their phones or hang a copy on their fridges to review whenever needed. Another great thing is that the written patient instructions will be pulled into the visit notes. During the follow-ups, it's a great objective measure to remind the patients of what I wrote previously and reinforce utilizing this resource.

EHR Workflow During the Encounter

By the time I enter the patient's room, I would have the old note (for existing patients) copied to a new note, and I would have already selected the labs and parts of the imaging and pathology reports to include. I would also take snippets of the radiology images or insulin pump/continuous glucose monitor reports and include them in the note. As I talk to the patient, asking about the interim events and how they're doing, I'll fill this information in the (Interval History) under the HPI.

I'll review the outside records for new patients before the visit. Previously, it was scanned in the chart, and reviewing it was difficult. Imagine being only able to see a page at a time; I couldn't scroll through the pages, and it wouldn't be easy to go back and forth with your notes in the EHR. I worked hard to update the protocol, educate the staff, and have them attached as PDFs that I can have side-by-side with the EHR note. You can easily adjust your screen size by pulling the title bar down and using any corner to resize it. I can scroll through the PDF on one half of the screen while having my note on the other half and typing or dictating directly before the visit.

I'll usually maintain eye contact with the patient while touch-typing whatever is relevant as we go through the history. I'll go next to editing the physical exam based on my findings, and then I'd usually stand by the patient's side and show them what I have in the labs, imaging studies (frequently pulling the pictures), or glucose reports. The patients are usually eager to be involved in my data assessment, actively participate in the analysis, and arrive at conclusions. It also makes it easier to agree on a shared plan.

Afterward, I edit the assessment and plan accordingly, and I'll type while saying it out loud to patients. I usually start by saying: "Let me tell you what I'll write down. You can access it through the portal; I'm not hiding anything." I usually write in the plan what I'll copy and paste under patient instructions. I'll order all the needed work-up to be done soon, if necessary, and before the upcoming follow-up visit, along with reconciling the medications. I'll finalize the instructions afterward with all these details.

When the patient leaves the room, I'm ready to finalize the note, place the charge, and prepare for the next patient. This is the usual rule that I'll do almost all the time. By the time the last patient leaves, I'm done with all the notes and charges for that day. In between the patients, I go through the inbox, messages, and results and aim to finish them by that time.

My clinic usually runs from 8 AM to 4-4:30 PM. I'm usually at the clinic from 7:45 AM to 8 AM and generally leave by 4-4:30 PM; I rarely stay till 5 PM. I almost always leave the office by that time with finished notes, charges, and a clean inbox. That's why such a clinic is a beautiful practice with a low chance of burnout. If you still need to get there, go through the foundational steps mentioned earlier in the book and build it one step at a time to reach this status.

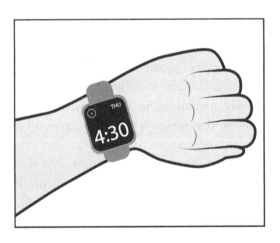

MD Efficacy

Efficient at work
Communicate with the patient and the EHR
simultaneously or within minutes of the visit

Effective everyday
All the notes for the day are finished at the same time
you are finished with clinic

6

PATIENT SATISFACTION

A satisfied customer is the best business strategy of all.
(Sam Walton)

We're in an era when patient satisfaction is critical. Many patients will get practice-initiated phone calls, messages, or email communications after each visit, asking about their satisfaction with the visit. This will frequently be publicly available. Also, patients can write their comments on Google Maps, Yelp, Facebook, Instagram, and TikTok, among many other social media platforms. This is in addition to the online patient support groups where they publicly discuss their experience. It's an exciting time to practice, and we should respect it. This is even more important if you have a private practice since consistent bad reviews can ruin it.

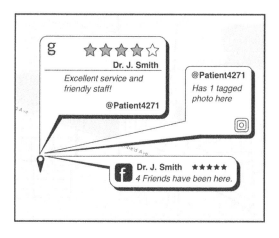

You need to be aware of some foundational pieces of knowledge. Dealing with people is enjoyable and rewarding, but it can get tricky. If you're in a leadership position, you're already aware of that. And sad enough, humans are frequently illogical. Many decisions are emotion-based rather than evidence-based. Let's dive deeper into it as it directly correlates with patients' assessments.

How Do We Make Decisions?

Our brains are so complex in their design. The cerebral cortex is responsible for high-functioning reasoning and decision-making. It tells the person this is the right thing to do and guides our actions. The limbic system is the heart of our brain, a beautiful part responsible for our emotions. During childhood, a dad will punish his kid for lying, so the limbic system will associate it with pain. Next time that kid considers lying, the pain experience will come up.

On the other hand, if you do well in an exam or publish a paper in a highly-ranked journal, you feel great about yourself. Your limbic system gets a dopamine high, and you feel terrific about it. You do your best to do the same again because it's a joyful experience. This beautiful design was intended to encourage good behaviors and discourage wrong behaviors. Unluckily, like the other parts of our bodies, it can get diseased and, sometimes, very diseased.

There are good ways to get these dopamine highs: Exercising, eating a healthy meal, hanging out with good friends, serving others in your community, or getting a good grade. There are shortcuts to reaching a far higher high, and because these highs are so good, people may get addicted quickly. These can range from video games, social media platforms (especially in gaining followers and likes), extreme shopping, extreme eating behaviors, and serial monogamy to smoking, vaping, drugs, sex, pornography, masturbation, and gambling.

A good question is, who wins the fight? Will the cerebral cortex or the limbic system win the battle? The sound reasoning or the emotions? I'm unsure about your experience, but I dealt with many people with addictions through my church services. The vast majority admitted that they were addicted and that it was bad for their lives, but very few could quit independently. The cortex functioned well, but the limbic system won the fight every time.

Why did I discuss all of that? This is not an addiction management session but rather to give you a heads-up on how our patients (and we) make decisions. A doctor could be a genius, have published 100s of papers, and have written many books, but needed a more effective and pleasant clinical encounter with a patient. A bad experience may result in a poor review, and the patient won't return to them. On the other hand, another doctor with limited funds of knowledge but excellent communication skills may easily win that specific patient, and they will do faithfully what their doctor would ask them to do. It's unlucky that we think we need to build more knowledge to help the patients when they'd listen to us if we have a whole different set of basic human and business skills that were not often integrated into our training.

Consider this as a diamond ring in a box. If you are working hard to buy the best ring you can get, you better go to the best shop, get a lot of advice, and ensure you get a beautiful one. When you gift it, will you put it in a beautiful box or a muddy and torn one? The norm is the former. If you follow the latter, the ring is still precious, but your efforts will be significantly underestimated. Think about your medical knowledge as the ring. It's expensive, precious, and has a high innate value. The box is your social skills. They're necessary to complete the package and ensure the whole experience is excellent.

Be Principle-Based

Before I start talking about techniques to help improve patient satisfaction scores, we need to agree on a shared foundation. Quick-fix approaches can help you get the patients' trust fast. Will these patients fully trust you with their care for the rest of their lives? Will they bring all their family members and friends to you? That's a whole other deal. There are crooked marketing people who can convince you to buy their products, but you'll never see them again. You may soon find you wasted your money and time, and sometimes, it's a significant loss.

The same analogy applies here: First, you want to have the correct principles, then improve your personality ethics and techniques to ensure the win of both short-term and long-term battles.

These principles are profound, and they will go to the foundations

- Love for your patients what you would love for yourself. Always put yourself in the patient's shoes and ask yourself, what would I like to do? If you think your offer is not the best, you may not want to offer it.

- Don't steal. Don't offer a treatment that will get you more income, but it's not the best for the patient. Return to the prior advice: if you don't accept it as a patient, don't push it.

- Don't accept a financial conflict of interest with another party trying to push their products in your practice. The same rule applies here. And thanks to the Sunshine Act, it became a mandated law for physician financial transparency. Transparency creates freedom, and it's beautiful. Even if you're getting paid less, you're doing the right thing, which is liberating.

- Know your specialty well and understand your limitations. If you don't know, ensure that you will be faithful in looking it up or reaching out to those who know. Make high-quality patient care your priority since it will pay off later and your patients will trust you.

- Remember that you are dealing with sick people. They wouldn't need a physician if they were in perfect health. Have sympathy and understand their weaknesses. I'll support, empathize, and kindly show the issue clearly. It's up to them to accept the options as they have the free will to choose. And they are the ones who will deal with the consequences of their decisions, not me.

A Smile

Patients like to feel welcomed in the clinic, and isn't it great when you go to a place and feel that people are happy to have you there? A sincere smile conveys that feeling of being welcomed right away. It's also a universal language. Even people from different cultures and languages will clearly understand it.

On the other hand, a grumpy face will convey a message entailing that I'm not happy to see you, and it'll be great if you leave as soon as possible. We don't want to share such a negative message with our patients or anyone else.

There's an interesting phenomenon: When you start smiling, you'll feel happier. The other person will likely smile as well. As I mentioned earlier, I'm not a big fan of personality ethics and quick fixes but rather principle-based approaches. If the foundation is the cake, you want to do your best to have a high-quality product. Then, the personality ethic is the beautiful icing so that it also looks great. Both have to combine for the best experience for the patient and yourself. Being a physician, you already worked so hard on the foundational part to be who and where you are. When I started digging deeper into understanding different personalities and building that foundation, this is when adopting these quick fixes helped so much.

The Name

The dearest word for anyone's ears and heart is their name. It brings a different perspective when you call someone by their name compared to a generic title like "sir, doc, buddy, ...". Make sure you call your patients by name as it brings a nice personal touch. Remembering the family members' names will also be great so they will appreciate you even more. The same applies to all you contact at work, in your neighborhood, or frequent shopping places. Remembering names can go a long way.

I saw a few of my attending physicians who were gifted in this perspective. They'll remember the names of all the family members of a patient they saw six months ago. I didn't get this gift at all. I can remember many names, but I need to take my time after frequent exposures for them to settle and regular visits to ensure I won't forget them. So, I decided not to rely on my memory and keep them written in the HPI. And if they're doing an extraordinary job or have a particular personal interest, I'll also write it down. While reviewing the chart before entering the exam room, all the details will come seamlessly to me, and the visit will be far more friendly.

I want to clarify that my workaround is not to fake my care and personalization since I genuinely do care. I understand my limitations while wanting to provide the best personable care. You need to find a solution that fits your workflow. Many patients would be glad I remembered their family members' names and their previously discussed personal details. If it's vital for them, it will also be vital for me. I care about them, their experience, and care.

Listen

I'm unsure if it was a part of medical training, but physicians tend to jump to conclusions fast. It may also be the way of our many exams where you read a few sentences and want to decide the answer immediately. It takes effort to resist interrupting the patients when they are talking so we can provide our expertise right away. In addition, some patients sway into side talks irrelevant to the discussed visit issue, but this may be vital for them.

I'm a big believer in the middle ground. We need to allow the patients adequate, uninterrupted time to talk and ensure they're not holding any vital information. Before I move to the physical exam, I'll ask: Is there anything else you want to share? Am I missing anything before moving forward? Also, after discussing the whole plan and writing the instructions, I'll ask again: Is there anything important you would like me to address today?

On the other hand, I believe we should be the moderators for the clinical encounters. We're the ones who should guide the conversations. If a patient started to tell a long story about a family member, entirely irrelevant to the encounter, I'd politely drive the conversation back to our topic soon enough. Some sociable patients won't mind talking for 2 hours about their social life.

No Blaming

Pride and self-centeredness are very prevalent. You can see babies being self-centered, where everything is "mine." They learn how to share as they grow, but it takes time. If you start blaming an adult, you can see the various defense mechanisms you learned about in Psychology 101. Remember denial, rationalization, projection, and displacement, among several others? You want the visit to be something other than a battle of blaming the patient and them defending themselves. It wastes the visit's time and you won't reach your goals either.

In addition, we have weaknesses and shortcomings in many perspectives. They are just different things than our patients at these points in time. Also, they're more vulnerable in the patient seat, while we are in the physician seat, frequently considered as judges. Having this type of sympathy and sharing that we all have weaknesses may change the visit dynamic when they can open up and share their weaknesses. This can be the perfect time to use the healing hands and kindly help them through the pains of recovery.

Be Sincere

I don't think I can emphasize this enough: The patients can feel your heart and whether you genuinely care about them. It would be best to be sincere during the clinical encounter, share their pain, and care about their health. The idea of "fake it till you make it" is terrible; you'll lose your patients' trust, business, and positive reviews. Start with your inside, ensure it's right, and the outside will be great.

A Strong Culture

A pleasant culture should be for all the clinic staff, not just a single person's attitude. Your patient will start the encounter with the reminder before the visit, the front desk person, medical assistant, yourself, the checkout person, and the triage if they call in between the visits. Systems don't work by a single person; you need to have everyone on the same page.

The first step is to work on yourself to be humble and open to feedback. If you can say, "I may be mistaken," it will encourage others to open up and share their concerns. It will also push them to be humble and accept your feedback. Regular meetings and being explicit about these values will help align the efforts. It would be best if you had the guts to share heart-to-heart personal feedback with those who need it. Never blame someone in front of others, as it will back-fire. Also, pay attention to issues before things get out of control. Be prompt and on top of your game.

Reflection and Self-Assessment

If it's not your nature, start practicing these pieces of advice. Start with one at a time, the one you think you need the most. Put a reminder on your phone at regular intervals to assess how you're doing. Maybe start with a nightly check-in and reflect on the day. How did you do? You may begin journaling to keep track of your progress. The more serious you work on it, the better you will get.

If I were in your shoes, I'd take objective measures to assess my improvement. How many hours am I working on average before or after work hours? What are my current average patient satisfaction scores? How many inbox messages and prescriptions am I getting per day? How many patients do I see per day? How is my average productivity per day? Assess whatever is relevant to you now and regularly in the future, monthly, for example, and see if you're heading in the right direction. You may keep a dedicated document for your baseline and follow-up data. And if not, you are best to assess why or maybe reach out for help if needed.

MD EFFICACY

EFFICIENT AT WORK
GENUINE, SINCERE, WARM INTERACTION WITH PATIENTS
RESULTS IN HIGHER PATIENT SATISFACTION

EFFECTIVE EVERYDAY
YOUR PRACTICE WILL FLOURISH AS CURRENT PATIENTS
RECOMMEND FUTURE PATIENTS

7

MANAGING THE INBOX

The most effective way to do it is to do it
(Amelia Earhart)

In the outpatient world, the inbox is a primary concern. Many patients may have problems, occasionally frequent, in-between visits. After the HITECH Act and the mandate for the EHRs to have portal systems, many patients got access to these portals, which is beneficial in many aspects. The more patients you see, the more these communications will happen, which can get overwhelming. Let's discuss some aspects of managing your inbox.

Is it a Burden?

Many things in life depend on how you view them. When I look at a busy inbox, I often think of my blessings: a busy clinic and many patients to care for. I'm not underestimating the burden but highlighting another perspective we shouldn't forget.

I encourage all my patients to get portal access. It makes

communication much easier and less bothersome. As a patient, I'd send a portal message to my primary care in a minute rather than waiting on the phone for 15-20 minutes to speak to someone I am unsure will address my concern. It also allows the staff to get to the message at a time convenient to them and review the chart before responding.

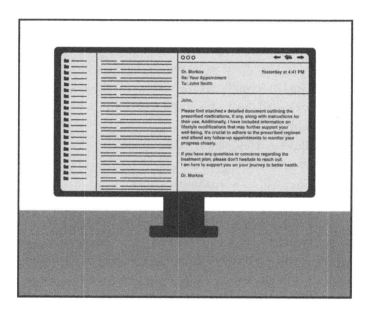

Messages

The portal messages are a safe place for patients to share their concerns. I know there are CPT charge codes for portal messages, but these charges may discourage the patients from sharing their concerns.

Where I practice, I'm blessed to have licensed practical nurses (LPNs) who filter these messages, learn how I categorize them, and they're able to triage them accordingly. This is critical to maintaining your sanity in a busy practice.

I have three broad categories

1. Simple questions. They can review my last note and answer accordingly. They don't need to inform me about them at all.
2. Long messages or patients who have several concerns. They should reach out to that patient and recommend arranging a sooner visit. This will provide the patient with the best service, address all their issues during that visit, and avoid overwhelming me with 10-20 minutes to review all the details and respond with a lengthy reply.
3. Short and few concerns that require my attention, and they're unable to respond to them. They will forward these messages to me.

I am also transparent with the patients on these regulations. Suppose a patient sent a long message previously. In this case, I'll respectfully let them know that I'm unable to respond to these long messages and that it's better to keep their concerns for the visit or arrange a sooner visit if needed. I also set some expectations: I don't review glucose logs or order labs between visits. I know my limitations and what I can and cannot manage.

Labs

My advice for you, especially if you're a lab-dependent specialty, is to establish your practice around pre-ordering labs before the visits. The goal is for patients to get their labs done a few days before the visit to be ready for discussion during the appointment. The patients will maximize the benefit from the visit as you can ask all the relevant questions based on the recent labs, explain them, and have a detailed agreed-upon plan before they leave.

On the contrary, if you order the labs for the patients to get after leaving the visit, you'll have to review them afterward. You may often have more questions and a modified plan to convey. Will you call the patient? Or ask your medical assistant (MA) or nurse to contact them? Will they get back to you for additional data or questions? And the cycle keeps getting longer. I wouldn't say I like that and try to avoid it at all costs.

I usually order the next visit's labs during the present visit. I'll set the time frame for these labs around the planned next visit. This will ensure that if the patient goes in a week or two for another doctor's labs, mine will be excluded. I'll also write clearly in the patient instructions section to get the labs done before the upcoming visit, along with the relevant instructions for these labs.

For the patients who miss these instructions, I'll mention that I'll let them know via a portal message or a mailed letter how their labs are doing. Also, if there are significant issues, I may need to see them sooner for further discussion.

Phone Calls

I find phone calls with patients between visits a challenge. Patients may not answer, and you leave a voice message. As the task is not over, you will need to call them again later, and the item wasn't checked from your to-do list. The patients may have additional questions for you and your planned 3-minute call could take 10-15 minutes.

I also do my best to minimize the phone calls for myself

and my staff. As I'm proactive in inviting all my patients to the EHR portal system, we encourage electronic messages and communication as much as possible. Most of my patients will get their labs before the visits, minimizing the lab follow-up phone calls after the visits. Also, providing detailed written patient instructions decreases confusion about what to do after the visits.

Of course, there will still be inevitable phone calls, but they are far more manageable than other less efficient practices.

Prescriptions

We should save our precious time on issues that can be held perfectly well by well-trained nurses or MAs. Your homework is to have a clear and comprehensive plan for medication refills and substitutions. This will give autonomy to your staff to do them automatically and clear your inbox of all the refills except for the controlled substances, which is reasonable.

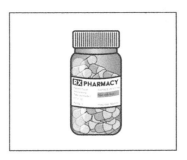

Where I practice, I'm lucky to have an excellent service line leader who worked this list of substitutions, and all the faculty will sign off on them annually. If Lantus is not covered, all the approved alternatives are there for the staff, and they'll check what's covered and send the comparable dosing. The same goes for prior authorizations where they'll run them in the background and fill out the forms, and I'll only sign whenever needed. This excellent setup makes sure that your valuable time will be dedicated to where your expertise is.

Another important thing is how many refills to give. Our general practice rule is to provide refills up to a year after the last patient's visit. This is an excellent rule for compliant patients; you do the refills once yearly and save staff time during that whole year. However, it can be hazardous for patients inconsistent with their visits, especially those having severe uncontrolled diabetes or patients on high doses of methimazole or diuretics. Some patients will abuse the rule and show up only once yearly despite my initial request to see them in a 6-week or 3-month interval. I will usually provide medication supplies for these patients until the planned next visit only. My staff members know my rules for such patients when they call for refills, and they will provide supplies up to a month after the recommended scheduled visit in my note. They will also ensure that a visit is arranged by that time. If they missed it, no more supplies until they return since it's unsafe.

Reminders

This feature is handy, especially for patients with concerning work-up or if I need to remind myself to follow up on something. I'll schedule a reminder to appear at the expected date and time. It assures that I won't rely on my memory or an outside reminder system but one directly linked to the patient's chart.

I'll also use it for patients with significant uncontrolled labs who get testing done before their scheduled visit. I'll schedule the reminders to show up the day after that visit to ensure they are reviewed and cared for.

Overwhelming Inbox

Life gets in the way sometimes, and occasionally, the inbox is overwhelming and extremely busy. It is not uncommon after long weekends, off days, and annual vacations that the inbox gets flooded by tons of needs that necessitate hours of work.

Our hard work as clinicians is to ensure that this will be the exception rather than the rule. If you work on implementing the above-mentioned strategies, the flooded inbox will slowly improve and eventually become very manageable.

MD Efficacy

Efficient at work
Manage inbox tasks in a systematic and timely fashion using reminders as prompts. Staff can easily assist here

Effective everyday
Eliminate overflow of incoming information so you can focus on your current priority

8

ESTABLISH A WORKFLOW

The best way to predict your future is to create it.
(Abraham Lincoln)

Workflow management improves efficiency, efficacy, and satisfaction for you, your staff, and your patients. You're getting what you need on time, so you're not going back to your staff with issues or frustrations, and the patients are happy to be in and out quickly with everything they need.

Visit Notifications

Most current EHR systems can text or call patient reminders before the visits. The complexity of the underlying workflow can vary widely. At one end of the spectrum, it can be a simple text and request to call the office for cancellations. On the other end, it allows canceling and rescheduling the visit while offering this visit in the background to the wait-list patients.

As the core of an outpatient practice is the clinic visits, this notification system directly impacts the show-up rate. It's worth the investment.

The timing of the notifications will depend on your patient population and clinic statistics. You want to achieve a middle ground between insufficient and overwhelming notifications. You don't want the system to call, text, and email simultaneously before the visit since that's too much. As a patient, receiving the three notifications combined is annoying. It is paramount to respect the patient's preferences and have an easily navigable system to notify them, preferably by their preselected method. I suggest only two notifications before the visit, a week and 1-3 business days beforehand. The second alert should coincide with how efficient your clinic is in filling white space "empty slots." If your staff or system can fill them within 24 hours, doing it one business day beforehand makes sense. But if it takes them five days to fill the slots, you need to improve that significantly and consider the second notification to be around that time till it gets better.

Consider adding a few details to the notification message, like the arrival time rather than the actual visit time. A suggested reasonable time is 15 minutes for established patients and 30 minutes for new patients to allow for completion of the relevant paperwork and time for the MA to room them and get the vitals and needed information.

Upon Arrival

The front office team needs to understand the specifics related to your specialty. For an Endocrinology practice, patients with diabetes may have CGMs and insulin pumps. The staff should ask about it routinely when checking them in, asking for the devices, and uploading them so that they are ready by the time I walk into the patient's room. You're the best to determine which person does what. It can be the front office downloading them, MA, or another assigned person, based on your clinic's dynamics and by trial and error.

There are some technicalities that may or may not be relevant to you, but I will mention them as they may be valuable for some. You can download the various reports as PDFs or order/print and save them as PDFs. I recommend having a secure drive where these reports can be saved. In my current EHR, the staff can attach the PDF in a message and save it to the chart. I specifically requested that the message doesn't get sent to me. These patients are already in the clinic, and I'll see them in a few minutes. Why clutter my inbox when I review it anyway? I don't need additional unnecessary messages or clicks.

Rooming

You may decide to follow the visit times for patient rooming, but I found the concept of first-come, first-serve very valuable and effective. For example, a patient scheduled at 2 PM may show up at 1:30 PM while the 1:40 PM patient shows up at 1:50 PM, 10 minutes late (and 25 minutes late for the arrival time). If you respect the visit times, the 1:40 PM will be roomed first and will likely be ready by 2 PM, which is 20 minutes late. On the other hand, if you allow the staff to room those who arrive first, the 2 PM will be roomed by 1:40 PM, and you can finish seeing them by the time the other late patient is ready. My rule of thumb in the clinic is that whoever shows up first will be roomed first. It's the most efficient system to allow you to decrease the wait times for most patients and finish on time.

As the MA starts rooming the patient, they will do their routine and checklist. The key is its components. What do you want your MA to do? You want to decrease your workload to focus on the relevant clinic issues and delegate the less demanding issues to them. In my current workflow, the MA will get the vital signs, write the chief complaint, review all the medication history, assess the need for refills, and ask if there have been any major events since the last visit.

There was definitely a need for workflow adjustment. When I used a different EHR and could seamlessly copy the old note to a new one, I didn't need anyone to write my chief complaint. However, in the current workflow, I must select the visit's diagnoses before I can copy the old plan to the new note. If I don't select all of them, I need to close the old note, go to the problem list, select the missing diagnoses, and repeat the cycle by opening the old note and copying the data. It isn't efficient to keep going back and forth.

Reviewing the medications can be tedious while not mentally demanding, so you can delegate it. However, prescribing medications and ensuring that the dispensed amount, especially for insulin, suffices is an important decision, and the physician should do it. Also, history taking and physical exam are core clinical aspects that we're suited for. I won't delegate them to the staff for the endocrinology specialty.

No Shows

There are several angles to view and various approaches to handle no shows. First, from a patient standpoint, life events happen, and our lives are likely hectic. Also, the patients' memory may need additional help, and we all forget sometimes. If we were in the shoes of everyone, we would find excuses for everyone. On the other hand, when you know that a visit is important and there will be significant consequences if you are a no-show, I trust that you will make every effort and remember to go early and never miss it. If you know that something will interfere with that, you will call the office once you learn about it and make sure you reschedule that visit before the requested deadline. I think this is the real key.

One of my colleagues came up with a bright idea. If a patient is 5 minutes late, the front office will call them and convert their visit to a virtual one if they're agreeable. The patients often forgot their visits and weren't intentionally planning to miss them. This approach decreased her no-show rate by 30%, a significant improvement by a simple intervention.

For patients who cancel on the same day of the visit or the day before, especially if over the weekend, their slot may need to be filled. On the other hand, your triage may be getting many calls for urgent needs. They are best-suited to arrange same-day visits for these patients and empowering them to do this is critical. Also, having an automated or manual waitlist can help get these patients in sooner and make the most of your available clinic time. Some of my patients need labs every four weeks, sometimes sooner, and I know I don't have availability then. There are several challenges: I don't want to manage labs and medications between visits, yet it is medically necessary to see them. I don't want them to be frustrated that I'm asking for a particular follow-up that is not available. My current approach is to be clear up-front that my visits are limited in this time interval, get the first available appointment, and still get the labs in the requested time range. The checkout staff learned to add them to the waitlist, and I will message them once the lab results are in to put such patients at the top of the waitlist for last-minute cancellations. Virtual visits are beautiful here as they can fit the last-minute arrangements and don't interfere significantly with the patients' plans. These patients are the most ready for their visits because they had all the requested pre-visit work-up done.

The concept of boundaries is a necessity for the success of your practice. The consistent implementation of pre-defined consequences will assure long-term success and minimal confusion. It is crucial that the patients clearly understand the implications of late arrivals and no-shows. Reinforce it, also, by having it hung in the waiting area. The front office personnel may need to explain it to the new patients verbally, and they sign it as well. In the policy you draft, make sure you highlight the important parts in bold and between white spaces. Don't bury them in the middle of long paragraphs. Your responsibility is to implement it consistently. The staff will be confused if you're inconsistent or lenient. Reasonable exceptions are okay, but they should be infrequent. The exception can't be the rule. Otherwise, revisiting it to match your comfort level would be best.

Examples of such policies I suggest

- Patients may not be seen if they arrive 15 minutes past the arrival time.
- A new patient missing two visits can't arrange future visits.
- An established patient missing three visits in 2 years will be discharged.
- A no-show letter with the policy details will be sent after every no-show.
- A $50 charge will be applied for every established patient no-show and $75 for every new patient. This is the patient's direct responsibility; it won't be charged to their insurance; they can't arrange a replacement visit until they pay it. Some institutions, like mine, may opt not to implement it, but I believe it is important to ensure accountability.
- A cancellation will be honored if it is before 48 business hours of the visit. Otherwise, it will be considered a no-show.

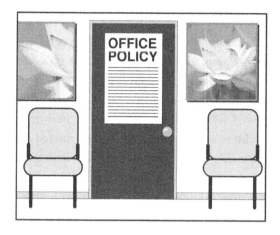

Between the Visits

Medication refill requests and prior authorizations (PAs) are a routine part of all practices. Many of the medications are expensive and very frequently require PAs. They require many hours for review and completion and don't generate direct revenue. It needs wisdom to ensure the job gets done efficiently while being careful about the resources.

From one standpoint, the physician's time is the most precious, and I'll ensure it's not wasted with silly messages and questions. Insurance companies change their coverage frequently, and the requests for medication exchanges are endless. A well-written protocol for medication exchanges can empower the staff to do them independently. When they're in doubt, they should reach out, but from your stand-point, encourage them to use the protocol whenever it's appropriate. Also, make sure this protocol gets updated annually and as needed. You may dedicate a readily acces-sible document to add your notes in real-time as ideas come so that when you revisit it, this resource will have all you need to update it. It's a vital need for your practice.

For the regular medication refills, I do my best to minimize the work for the staff. I provide a yearly supply for compliant patients to ensure this won't be an issue for the patients or the staff. At a glance, while looking at the old note, I can tell if the patient has been consistent with their visits or not. I write the follow-up interval in every note, for example, follow-up in 3 months. If they missed a visit, I'd write (last visit + date; example: last visit 1/2022) to remind myself how the patients followed up previously. For such patients, I provide refills until the next visit, and my staff members know they won't refill medications past a month of the scheduled visit. If the patient misses their visit, they have to arrange a sooner one. If they got the one-month refill and are still not seen, no refills would be provided till they come for a visit. It's a safer practice since many of the medications we prescribe need monitoring, and we're liable as we are the prescribers. We are the leaders here and shouldn't do something we're uncomfortable doing. From a financial standpoint, our time is expensive, so we can't afford to do that much free work without the expected reimbursement.

For the paperwork, like filling out forms including the Family and Medical Leave Act (FMLA), I will teach the staff how to review my last notes and fill them accordingly. If they don't know or have a particular issue, I'll take the longer path of reviewing the last note together, and they'll do it accordingly. You do it once, and they'll do it many times afterward, eventually making your life easier. I don't fill out disability paperwork and will be clear upfront about this rule.

Communication

I trust you frequently need to communicate with your MA, front office personnel, and triage nurses during the regular clinic day. They also need to reach out to you for questions. It can be time-consuming if you're chasing them, and they are also doing so. If you don't find them, it's a failed attempt that you may need to repeat. It was a dream come true when I got exposed to communication programs, like Microsoft Teams and Jabber, that your practice already has or can quickly adopt. These applications run in the background of the same computer you use for the EHR. You will get a notification with every message you get and can respond immediately. Also, you can share your concerns right away so the initial job is done. You can also track the messages and see which one you need to follow up on.

Continuous Quality Improvement

Improving your workflow is a continuous process, not a one-time thing. It needs awareness of what is going around you, the ability to recognize issues (we are experts here), and brainstorming on how to solve them. If you discuss the issues with the responsible team members, they can be a great resource on the available solutions. Trying something out for a while and then reassessing the process can be valuable to appraise those who thought and implemented the change. Calendar entries are valuable when we have many issues on our plate at baseline.

During my master's degree in healthcare informatics, I chose to do a practicum in my division. I compared the no-show rates in patients scheduled at remote intervals, to be seen in 9 to 12 months, to those scheduled at shorter intervals, 2 to 3 months. The initial hypothesis was that the former wouldn't show up as often as the latter, which makes sense. But this is not what I found. The remote interval patients weren't different from the other group and occasionally were more committed. I used the same skillset in my previous retrospective studies of data gathering and statistical analysis, but for workflow management it led to valuable data that made an impact.

Virtual Desktops

This is a bit more technical, but it's an important concept to understand. Your regular computer is a traditional environment where everything is kept locally; you naturally can't access it remotely unless you specifically set it up. On the other hand, a virtual desktop is located remotely, and your monitor is just a port to pull it. You can exit that port and open it seamlessly on another one. The system and your applications are running in the background, and you have access to everything.

In addition, you're frequently automatically logged in to the default browser with your work email. Saving passwords there can make logging into your various accounts more efficient. Even when the desktop is restarted after a long idle time, your passwords remain there as they're linked to your account, thus one less thing for you to think about and memorize.

This is critical as it's the current trend in my EHRs. Virtual desktops provide the luxury of pulling everything you have open on any computer at any point in time. It can also allow you to securely save your frequently used and important documents in a secure space.

In some systems, like mine, you can use the virtual

desktop or the standalone EHR when using the work-provided laptops. If this is your circumstance, I strongly encourage you to use your virtual desktop and save all your files and passwords. You don't want to add another techno-logical hassle, and this was designed to improve your life. Consider asking your informatics team to check if it is an available option for you.

Helpdesk Tickets

Technological issues will continue, no matter how great the system is. This is just the nature of computer codes. Know that there is always a chance for improvement. If you don't let the responsible team know about your issues, they will never know. Giving up and following a workaround is easy, but it doesn't help anyone, including yourself. I'm not asking you to fight every battle since some are not worth it. But when it's important and frequent, you need to raise your voice.

I found my Helpdesk team responsive to emails. Although there's a formal ticket submission system, it's tedious and not user-friendly. On the other hand, I can draft an email and include a screenshot of the issue carrying the patient's name and medical record number in less than a minute. I can easily do it through my workflow without significant interruption. It's a great middle-ground, and occasionally I achieve great success.

Let me tell you a story when I felt I made an impact. We have a process to attach images to the notes, either pasting or browsing for the photos. After a few months of using the system, the "paste" button stopped working. I submitted a ticket, and the first response was, why don't you save the photo and use the browsing functionality? This wasn't a satisfactory response since the workaround was tedious and would add at least five more clicks with every encounter. I asked for escalation and a fix of the root cause. It was a code issue, and they promised to fix it with the next upgrade, which they did. It was still functioning well until I wrote this book. In this instance, persistence was rewarded.

MD Efficacy

Efficient at work
Clear consistent communication, in person and virtually, ensures a functioning clinic

Effective everyday
A mostly low stress, supportive environment ensures staff and patient satisfaction

9

SET YOUR BOUNDARIES

You can't control your circumstances, but you can control your response to them.
(Tony Dungy)

L ife is full of beautiful things around us, and we have many communities where we can be active. Examples include family, work, community, and church or religious institution, if any, among many others. Our level of investment in each of them depends on how much we get rewarded and how far we would like to be involved. My work is busy in many aspects: clinical, research, teaching, and administration. I am also deeply involved with my family and church community, and both consume much time. When there are many demands, you learn the need to place boundaries, or you will reap unwanted consequences. To maintain your sanity, let's focus on those boundaries at work and a few outside of work.

Department Leadership

There are many leadership styles, ranging from the auto-cratic model on one end to the Laissez-Faire on the other. In the autocratic model, you can't oppose the leader. They follow the rule of my way or the highway. On the other hand, in the Laissez-Faire model, the leader doesn't have a say; the followers are the actual leaders. This depends strongly on the personality of the leader and their experience. You can have a good sense of their style during the initial interview as a new hire or during their recruitment meetings. They also will affect the department's culture and way of interaction.

Leaders have their agenda, which can benefit you but is sometimes harmful. Can you say "No, I can't do it" if needed? I'm not reassuring you that it will be honored every time, but sometimes, it can save your life. For example, an available administrative position will cause you to have several after-hour meetings interfering with your family's commitments, and it'll provide 10% additional revenue. That's a no for me, and I would nicely say, "No, I can't do it," without hesitation or guilt.

Sometimes, the rules come from high up in the corporation and will be enforced. Also, some decisions must be made as critical steps of the division's vision. That's why you need to pick your battles and fight the good fight. It's exhausting if you fight every opposing issue, and it will drain your energy and time. It will likely leave you frustrated and sore as you cannot win them all. However, it's also unhealthy to be obedient and people-pleasing, never able to say no so that you don't harm anyone's feelings. An analogy from the old days is that you'll be like a city with no walls or fences. All the foreign armies can come anytime, steal whatever they want, and leave. It's unprotected.

A good fight has two aspects: it is necessary for your mission and values, and you can win. Patience and persistence are essential virtues that you will need to follow. The first discussion is not the end of the battle. You will need to be consistent and firm until the issue is over. I remember a proposal from the senior leadership about changing the compensation plan for our division, among others, that would have a significant negative impact, at least in the short term. Interestingly, many cared a lot, but no one stood up to talk. I could feel their struggling boundaries. I recall meeting with the service line leader, division chairman, department chairman, and the institution's senior vice president. It was an important aspect, and I was determined it would be a good fight. It would be best to learn how to discuss, ensure a safe discussion environment, and maintain the language of respect since these are critical to avoid losing your battle. An elevated pitch of voice or anger wouldn't be permitted.

Through the years, I rejected committee memberships, administrative positions, and additional clinical work that didn't align with my vision and plan. On the other hand, I asked for extra support and insisted on new hires that would benefit the clinical work. One needs wisdom, guidance, and experience to know what is right and what is not. Also, having the ability to say no guilt-free and knowing the right time to say yes can help you so much.

I was lucky to have great leaders who encouraged me to say no and supported me when I said it. Great leaders are hard to find, but when you see them, you learn a lot, and they can support you significantly in your career path. You learn a lot from every interaction, and their responses practically apply their concepts. By definition, if the leaders are great, it's because of their principles.

Support Staff

The nurses and MAs are hired to help make your life smoother and more productive. A good, friendly relationship with your staff is excellent, but they're not your friends. If you sent a message to them asking to call the patient and they decide to send them a portal message or a letter, they dismissed your request. You just affirmed their action if you saw it and didn't talk to them about it. The same applies to prior authorizations, patient-requested forms, inbox triage, and whatever you assign them to do.

Consistency and predictability are necessary to avoid confusion. For example, we have nurses triaging the physicians' inboxes, and whatever they can handle won't be sent to us. My nurse knows that if a patient sends a long message, arranging a sooner visit is needed to allow the time to discuss their concerns. When they started working with me,

I met them and clearly stated my expectations. I got eight long messages in my inbox in the first week of their work. I replied to all of them to arrange sooner visits. The messages were down to four the following week, and by their first-month mark, it was one message per week. Now, if they send a long message to me, they'll summarize their concern in 1-2 lines after stating (I know that you would like a sooner visit). They understood what I wanted. My advice is to be consistent and respond right away. Consistency in teaching and defining the work territory of your staff is your best path to a less stressful workplace.

If a particular staff member isn't up to their job level, you may need to ask for a substitute. I remember having an MA who spent 15 to 20 minutes asking for history and having social chats with the patients when I had a full clinic and four other patients waiting to be roomed. I talked to them in several one-on-one meetings and they didn't change. I spoke to the clinic manager, who talked to them, but there was no improvement. I insisted on hiring another person and the leadership successfully complied. It will be best to confront people in a safe environment, ask for what you need, and learn to go through the appropriate hierarchy to get things down. It will be best not to skip your direct manager since it can backfire.

Patients

We're practicing medicine in an era when we receive regular reports of the patients' experience and scores comparable to hotels and restaurants. The quality of my service is not assessed by the percentage of thyroid cancer patients in remission or the well-controlled Graves' disease patients but by how pleased the patients are from the clinical encounter.

This adds a very different perspective on how we should run the practice. It adds the requirement to be pleasant and people-pleasing to ensure good feedback.

I believe in being delightful and learning the skills to achieve that. I found it very interesting that when you set the expectations upfront, the patients won't have issues following the rules if you're consistent every time and don't change them.

Examples of these expectations include:

- For your safety, I don't review glucose logs or adjust insulin doses between visits. I want to discuss these glucose readings with you as your input will significantly affect my decision. This always necessitates a visit.
- Although I can access the continuous glucose monitor data on the cloud, I cannot review it regularly. If you have concerns before the upcoming visit, please arrange a sooner one.
- I don't order labs between visits. For a new diagnosis of Graves' disease, I need to see you every month with labs a couple of days before the visit. I'll review them and adjust the dose during the visit.
- Please get your labs done before the visit, and we'll discuss them during the visit. This will make the best use of your time during the visit.

I see some of my colleagues receiving 50-60 portal messages daily. They wake up at 4:30 a.m., start work at 6:30 a.m., one and a half hours before their clinic's start time, and take work home as they cannot finish it all during the work schedule. On the other hand, I start my clinic at 8 am and finish by the time my last patient leaves, around 4:20 pm. By the time I leave, all my notes will be done, charges placed, and all inbox messages and labs taken care of. I also can see more patients, and the patient satisfaction scores are comparable and very good. Healthy boundaries can save your life in the clinic.

Family

Physicians are among the brightest and most hardworking people out there. It requires much persistence, many hours of studying, and long years of schooling and training to reach where we are. It breaks my heart to see many divorced physicians, single moms and dads, and several who have children with addiction problems or significant failures in life.

Many of these great physicians were unable to say no. I hope you understand that the most difficult no is the one you tell yourself. And among those is to stop one of your desires or ambitions. I once read a beautiful quote: "If you want to go fast, go alone, but if you want to go far, go together." Some are so ambitious for their career achievement that they disregard their spouses and families. We are all free to make choices, but we'll reap the consequences. Maybe you'll be the division chief, CEO, or world-renowned expert, but a divorced one at age 43. You did it fast but became alone.

Amid this busy life, many of us have children to raise. These children are growing up in beautiful houses, riding fancy cars, and having families with prestigious societal positions. The early years of their childhood are critical to developing strong bonds that can help through the rough teenage years. It is unlucky that the early critical years of our children's lives are the same early critical years of our career development. There are some sacrifices that we'll need to make. Know that your decision will determine their outcome.

The encouraging point is that 20% of the work can lead to 80% of the outcome. Pick your essential battles up front, but ensure that the needed family time is sacred. No one can touch it. Your spouse and children will appreciate you for that, and in the long term, you'll achieve far more than if you sped up early on. Sometimes, a turtle can go further than a rabbit. I'm a perfectionist; although I pick only 20%, I do it very well, so I don't go back for revisions. Just select the right battles and do them well. If you don't do it right the first time, fixing the mistakes can take much more time and effort.

Faith

This section applies to your religious affiliations as well as community service. I have been involved and active at my local church since my early years. I started serving middle schoolers during my senior year in high school and continued serving since then. As the years went by, my responsibilities increased as well. Serving the Lord is very rewarding and adds significantly to spiritual well-being. It's also our responsibility to the next generation. The problem is that tasks can pile up fast and infringe on your personal life.

The church's leadership and management of services follow the same principles as managing tasks at work in an organization, just in the spiritual realm. Having vision, defined jobs, committed volunteers, and good leaders would be best. You need love, discipline in the implementation and follow-up, and excellent boundaries.

If you accept all the available tasks as a good servant of Christ, you'll burn out quickly, and your spouse and family may be negatively affected. If they are kind enough and understand how great of a servant/leader you are and don't have the good boundaries to tell you that this won't work, you may find out late that they are so burnt out due to your absence. The bigger problem is that, in many instances, you're feeding your pride in service rather than bringing fruits for the Lord.

Having healthy boundaries can go a long way, more than you imagine. If you understand your priorities and what you can do without infringing on your personal time, family life, and work, you're building yourself by working in the field of the Lord. Also, your family will appreciate that you're letting go of some things for their sake. This may also help control your pride by restraining you from shining so much in a place but forgetting your other essential priorities.

Wisdom in Boundaries

We have many beautiful aspects to enjoy, which all add to the beauty of our time on this earth. We may lose sight of this beauty when we convert them to achievable tasks and run from one achievement to another. We forget about the bigger picture and focus on the small things before us when we're advised to do one without neglecting the other.

We can't do everything in every aspect of our lives, we simply can't. We also have a limited time per day, week, month, year, and lifetime. That's why strategic planning and having a vision of what you want to be and to do should be clear. With every decision, you weigh it against this vision and mission, and based on that, you can make your decision easier and faster if you want to commit to this new task. Stephen Covey elaborated beautifully on these aspects in his book 'The Seven Habits of Highly Effective People' when he discussed starting with the end in mind and doing first things first.

It is easy to get distracted by the frequent little achievements. The design of our brains is fascinating, the science of behaviors and their modification is interesting, and it can be predictable, although complex. The most advanced artificial intelligence and machine learning programs are behind in the competition of the human brain despite following its footsteps in learning. The limbic system is where the heart of emotions resides. It gets a high from achievement and success and a low from a negative consequence or punishment. The little achievements give a quick high and satisfaction, and the person feels good. It's easy to get distracted by the fast results.

Persistence, perseverance, and delayed gratification are valuable virtues. During my high school years, my mind was set on the dream of being a successful doctor with a solid medical foundation. The path was clear, and I accepted that I'd start earning real money after 15 additional years of study and training. I could visualize my colleagues graduating in 4 years, earning high incomes, getting married, and having families while I followed the path of monasticism in medicine. Many people nowadays make similar choices and choose shortcut pathways. They want prestigious positions and good money while not spending long years of study and training. The virtues above are seeds that should be planted in the early years of life; don't go after the easy and short paths. The fruits are less beautiful than the lengthier and stricter way. I'm not saying not to work smart. I'm encouraging you to work hard in a smart way.

If the vision is set correctly on the right long-term goal and the heart coincides with the brain, then saying an emphatic no to the options that don't align with it will be easy. For example, I have an important upcoming exam in a couple of days. I'm aiming for an A+, and a colleague is inviting me to watch a sports game that will require 2 hours. That's an easy no, as the career path comes first. I would love to enjoy another game after finishing my exam. If a church leader asks me to deliver a talk at a Sunday morning meeting and I pre-arranged an outing with my family, that's another easy no, as family comes first. I can pick another talk on another day that doesn't collide with my family's plans.

Obstacles to Boundaries

Many people have difficulty setting healthy boundaries. Several issues can lead to that. There are different personality traits. Some of them, primarily the sociable and the perfection-seeker, can tend to be people-pleasing and have difficulty in setting good boundaries. They're fearful of the pain of rejection and isolation. It should be clear that everyone can control only themselves, and no one can control others' behaviors. Most people will understand and respect these boundaries. If the other person isn't mature enough to accept the no, they may elect to do one of several manipulations in an attempt to control the situation. The most common are avoidance, rejection, or withdrawal of love. The far less common but more severe ones include bad-mouthing, financial punishments, and even causing psychological or physical harm. You need to understand that it's a war for your freedom and not for free. You can only control yourself, not others. Fight the good fight and stand for your borders where no intruders are allowed.

Perfectionism and all-or-none rules can set you up for failure. Do you think you'll be an expert surgeon when holding the scalpel for the first time? The same applies to boundaries; it's like a muscle you're training. Start low and go slow since this is how you'll develop healthier boundaries daily without losing so much to unnecessary conflicts. You should also have a mentor who can set boundaries nicely and effectively. I'm a big believer in discipleship. The most challenging step is to find the right guide whom you'd like to reach their level in a particular virtue. Afterward, asking for guidance and following their advice can save you time and prevent many mistakes throughout the learning path, this is paramount.

MD Efficacy

Efficient at work

Saying "no" to a work request allows you to say "yes" to preferred work, family, or community priorities.

Effective everyday

Strong boundaries enhance your sense of self and allow you to be present for yourself and others.

AFTERWORD

I hope you found this book helpful and the tips I suggested here practical and doable. Please don't feel overwhelmed, and don't try to implement many simultaneously; this can cause significant confusion. If I'm in your shoes, start with a single improvement till you master it, and then you can add one at a time. Small changes can go a long way.

I'm hopeful that in future books, I'll address additional aspects of the lives of efficient physicians. Keep up your great work and substantial impact on your patients' lives.

For additional references and resources, please visit www.MDEfficacy.com. You can join the newsletter to receive useful tips and tricks. Please feel free to email me comments, suggestions, concerns, or questions at info@ MDEfficacy.com.

ACKNOWLEDGMENTS

I want to thank Dr. Samir Habib and Dr. Maher Rizkalla for reviewing this book and providing valuable, constructive feedback. Thanks also to Dr. Mary Salama and Dr. Fady Nashed for reviewing the manuscript and providing encouraging feedback.

I appreciate the professional help of Mary Todd in editing the manuscript, Mike Trent for the book cover and illustrations, Shadow Studio for the headshots, and Aryn Van Dyke for the marketing planning.

I would like also to thank the endocrinology faculty at Indiana University School of Medicine. I learned and continue to learn a lot from you. The division's leadership taught me how to have a vision and how leading by service should be.

I would also like to thank my fellows, residents, students, staff members, medical community, and patients. Their questions and needs sparked the ideas in this book and upcoming series.

ABOUT THE AUTHOR

Personal Background

Dr. Michael Morkos is an Assistant Professor of Clinical Medicine at Indiana University School of Medicine. He received his medical degree at Alexandria University School of Medicine in Egypt. He completed his internal medicine residency at John H. Stroger Jr. Hospital of Cook County and endocrinology fellowship at Rush University Medical Center, both in Chicago, IL. He earned a master's degree in clinical research at Rush University Medical Center and a master's degree in healthcare informatics at Indiana University. Dr. Morkos earned the American Board Certification in internal medicine, endocrinology, and clinical informatics.

Dr. Morkos has several interests besides medicine that ended up being the best fit for the idea behind his brand, MD Efficacy, to help other physicians improve their efficiency and productivity in clinics while maintaining excellent patient satisfaction scores. Some light is being shed below on the details.

Clinical Medicine

The core of a physician's scope of practice is helping patients using medical knowledge. Dr. Morkos strongly believes in clinical excellence as the core for achieving clinical efficiency and efficacy. His clinical practice is currently focused on thyroid disorders. He was the first physician to introduce thyroid radiofrequency ablation (RFA) in the state of Indiana, and he is one of the few physicians in the US to use spectral Doppler ultrasound in the initial assessment of patients presenting with thyrotoxicosis. Thyroid RFA is a novel, minimally invasive procedure to treat symptomatic benign thyroid nodules, small thyroid cancers, parathyroid adenomas, and metastatic lymph nodes in the neck.

Clinical Research

Dr. Morkos earned a master's degree in clinical research at Rush University Medical Center in 2017. He performed statistical analyses for all his studies, including descriptive and inferential analyses. He also developed and validated a logistic regression-based predictive model for the risk prediction of acute pancreatitis in patients with severe hypertriglyceridemia [1,2]. He believes a basic understanding of statistics is essential to assess the daily clinic operations and develop sound assessments to guide interventions.

Computer and Informatics Skills

Dr. Morkos has a long-standing passion for dealing with computers. He was the de facto clinical champion in guiding his colleagues on improving efficiency through shortcuts and interface improvements in the EHRs during residency, fellowship, and as a faculty member. He earned a master's degree in healthcare informatics from Indiana University in 2021 and the American Board Certification in Clinical Informatics in 2023.

Accounting and Business

Dr. Morkos aced the subjects of accounting and business during high school. Since then, these concepts have remained in the T accounts, profit and loss accounts, balance sheets, and break-even points. He has a special love for math, numbers, and quality improvement. They became an integral part of his planning and thought processes. These skills became critical in understanding and managing productivity and having reasonable projections.

Quality Improvement

There are always opportunities for improvement. Recognizing these chances, analyzing the root causes, brainstorming the options, implementing changes, and assessing the impact need unique skill sets. During residency training, Dr. Morkos was awarded the best idea and teamwork for a quality improvement project. He proposed and facilitated the implementation of many quality improvement initiatives during his practice. These are critical skill sets to ensure resisting inertia and improving the practice workflow, patient satisfaction, clinical efficiency, and productivity.

Understanding Human Psychology

The main scope of practice of Dr. Morkos is outpatient medicine, although he does monthly procedures and 6-8 weeks of inpatient service per year. Therefore, understanding how to deal with people, including patients, clinic staff, and clinic leadership, is a must to ensure smooth daily clinic operations and excellent impacts. Dr. Morkos enjoyed reading and understanding human psychology for years, and he is the guru at his church, along with a psychiatrist, in delivering psychology-related topics in adult and youth meetings. It is an art and a skill that all clinicians need to comprehend.

Counseling and Mentorship

Dr. Morkos is passionate about teaching and guiding others. He believes in the Socratic teaching philosophy, starting with questions to assess the audience level before building on it. Over the years, he enjoyed coaching many medical students, residents, fellows, faculty members, and Sunday school students. He is also interested in the art of public speaking, and his presentations are engaging.

Leadership

Dr. Morkos had several leadership positions at his local church, which has 450 families. He has been the secretary for the church's board of trustees since 9/2019, was the coordinator for the high school services 2021 – 2023, and is currently assisting in coordinating the Sunday school services at his church. He suggested and led several work-related projects as well.

Improving physicians' efficacy, productivity, efficiency, and well-being and maintaining excellent patient outcomes and satisfaction, necessitates unique skill sets besides solid medical knowledge. Dr. Morkos' mission is to dive deep into these various skill sets, elaborate on them, and help coach other physicians to improve their lives in the clinic.

∼

1 Amblee, A., et al., Acute pancreatitis in patients with severe hypertriglyceridemia in a multi-ethnic minority population. Endocrine Practice, 2018. 24(5): p. 429-437.

2 Morkos, M., et al., External validation of a predictive model for acute pancreatitis risk in patients with severe hypertriglyceridemia. Endocrine Practice, 2019. 25(8): p. 817-823.

Made in the USA
Las Vegas, NV
02 August 2024

93282098R00075